HIP
HOTELS

CITY

NEW EDITION • NEW HOTELS

HERBERT YPMA

HIP
HOTELS

CITY

NEW EDITION • NEW HOTELS

with 630 illustrations, 515 in color

Thames & Hudson

introduction

A trickle has turned into a stream. When the original version of this book came out a few years ago, the demand for somewhere different to stay was still a whisper. The mere presence of some Bauhaus furniture together with a groovy, unconventional bathroom was still enough to qualify as an interesting urban hotel experience, and for that guests were even prepared to forgive a lack of services. No pool? No gym? No room service? No sophisticated business facilities? No problem. Rather that than the 'no surprises' world of the Holiday Inn. The hotel industry in general didn't really take these amateur newcomers too seriously. After all, they reasoned, the business traveller will always put reliability ahead of innovation.

Don't bet on it. Three years later, it is clear that the mainstream hotel trade radically underestimated the demand for originality and personality. The tables have completely turned. These new urban Hip Hotels have left the global chains panting in their wake. With the opening of each new individual hotel in one of the world's capital cities, the standard is being raised a few notches, and not just in terms of design. The best food, the best in-house gyms, the snappiest, sexiest room service, the most inventive new features such as vacuum plumbing, web TV and in-room mini delis; in short, the most impressive array of facilities are now offered by hotels that were not too long ago considered the odd outsiders. Boutique hotels, design hotels, charming hotels – all these slightly diminutive labels seem not just laughably inappropriate but horribly out of date. Hip Hotels, particularly in the world's premier cities, now distinguish themselves not just by being individual but by being the best – bar none. One Aldwych in London, Amanjena in Marrakesh, the Manor in Delhi, Establishment in Sydney: all are new, and all are already the pace-setting hotels in their respective cities. Some, such as the Prince in Melbourne, have completely outgrown the traditional hotel model and morphed into something which, for want of a better description, can be described as a lifestyle location. The choice and the quality of one-off hotels, both large and small, is continually on the rise. And the winner of this on-going 'hipper' and 'better' competition is of course you, the traveller.

blakes hotel

Amsterdam really needed a hotel like this – a place as extraordinary as the city itself. The unique beauty of Amsterdam has its origins in the city's Golden Age, when, enriched by the success of its 136,000-strong fleet (no wonder there are no more forests), Holland was both a significant naval power and one of the most affluent nations in the world. One shipload of spices from Indonesia, or of porcelain from China, yielded enough profit to allow a merchant to retire in comfort for the rest of his life. There was quite literally an embarrassment of riches, and the staid, conservative, church-going burghers were almost forced to look for ways to spend their money. They were the world's first affluent, mercantile middle-class and, with or without guilt, they started to patronize on an unheard-of scale. Silversmiths, goldsmiths, cabinet-makers, painters and sculptors (some of whom had fled religious persecution in their native France), and of course architects were enlisted to create things of beauty – including many of the impressive buildings that still today stand along Amsterdam's canals. As always happens in any society swept by a tide of affluence, there were the rich and the very rich. The very rich built homes on the Keizersgracht, the

Emperor's Canal, where the houses are still more grand – more Palladian in shape and more symmetrical in design.

With an address on the Keizersgracht, Blakes Hotel couldn't be better located. And it has an architectural pedigree to match. Built in 1632 and designed by the then famous architect Jacob van Campen, this stone building was originally a theatre – a place illuminated by the plays of Molière and Shakespeare as well as concerts conducted by Vivaldi. But the Golden Age came to an end, and so did the building's life as a theatre – suitably dramatically in 1772, when it burned down in the middle of a show. All that was left after the inferno was the lovely neoclassical stone facade. Fifteen years later, the Catholic church acquired the site and adapted what remained of the original structure into a bakery to feed the city's poor and underprivileged.

As Blakes Hotel, it has once again – as designer Anouska Hempel likes to quip – returned to its former status as a theatre, this time starring her work. But however remarkable her contribution, it was, in terms of the work that had to be done, just the finishing touch. First the building had to be rescued from a state of advanced dilapidation.

Crumbling walls, a missing roof and a listed stone facade were the sum total of what the Dutch banker-developer had to work with when he decided to turn this piece of historic real estate into a hotel.

That said, inviting Anouska Hempel, a.k.a. Lady Weinberg, to tackle the interior design was a masterstroke. Her trademark signature of contemporary minimalism with a colonial Asian twist could have no better setting than Amsterdam. Holland still has a strong and enduring love affair with its former Asian colonies. This is apparent in Dutch cuisine. Even today, half a century after Indonesia's independence, Holland's favourite dishes are *nasi goreng*, *bami goreng*, and *rijstafel*. The East was, after all, the source of the great wealth that gave rise to the Golden Age, and thus it will always be associated with the pinnacle of achievement in Dutch culture.

At Blakes, Hempel has masterfully captured the resonance and style of Holland's colonial past in a thoroughly contemporary fashion.

The vivid natural colours of spices, the blue and white of Chinese porcelain, the texture of bamboo, and the black that once defined the wardrobe of every well-to-do burgher: such ingredients are reinvented and introduced with great flair to the various rooms and suites. There is a jade suite; a blue and white room; an all-white duplex with its bathroom on the beamed mezzanine floor and a Chinese-inspired mandarin room as living room; a papyrus-hung gallery divided into small private spaces; and a typically Dutch bricked inner courtyard. None of this design obscures the very Dutch and very stately architecture, nor does it leave any doubt what country you are in. Even the restaurant, which used to house the bakery ovens, has retained a sober, utilitarian atmosphere despite its unmistakably up-to-date interior. Blakes is a rare achievement: one of those few places that manage to strike a balance between historical pedigree and thoroughly modern attitude. In this respect, the city and the hotel are one.

address Blakes Hotel, Keizersgracht 384, Amsterdam 1016GB, Netherlands
t +31 (20) 530 20 10/17 **f** +31 (20) 530 20 30 **e** blakes@shl.com
room rates from NLG 475

seven one seven

Take the finest British aristocratic guest house and transplant it to the heart of one of the grooviest cities in Europe and you have Seven One Seven: an up-market, all-suite, continental inner-city version of the very best British bed and breakfast tradition.

The exterior reveals little. If it weren't for the brass plaque on the outside of this dark green, double-fronted Empire-style canal house it could easily be mistaken for the discreet residence of an old Amsterdam family. It doesn't look like a hotel on the outside, and nor does it on the inside. The 'lived-in' interior is an unexpected combination of antique and modern, African masks and classical torsos, books and walking sticks, Murano glass and cast-iron urns – exactly the kind of eclectic, unpredictable mix that might be found in an old English country house.

Some fifteen years ago Kees van der Valk, a Dutch fashion designer and decorator, came across an unforgettable bed and breakfast in Braemar, Scotland – a place where a gentleman dressed in a beautiful suit would serve high tea beside a roaring open fire in an interior of exquisite comfort and beauty. That discovery launched him on a creative mission to realize his own vision of the perfect guest house. He toyed initially with the idea of buying a château in the French countryside, but concluded that there were already too many such converted châteaux in France and not nearly enough interesting places to stay in Amsterdam.

So the search began for the right property. In June 1996 van der Valk found the type of house that real estate people in Amsterdam will assure you 'normally never comes on the market' – a large, listed building ideally situated on the Prinsengracht, one of the main canals in the heart of the old city. After negotiating to buy the stately 1810 building back from a group of property developers intent on dividing it into eight apartments, the real work began. The Empire-style building (so called because it dates back to the brief reign of Napoleon Bonaparte's brother as King of the Netherlands) had long ago undergone a disastrous conversion into offices. A fifty-strong team set to work, stripping and virtually reconstructing the entire property. And thus in just six months it was brought back to its former domestic grandeur, and in fine style.

All plasterwork for the new ceilings was done by a team from England (Stevenson's of Norwich), and antiques were found at auctions and fleamarkets all over Europe.

Suzannah the resident Irish setter features in a reworked oil portrait by Dutch artist Bob van Blommenstein

Carefully arranged throughout the hotel are African artifacts from Tribal Art, an antique shop on nearby Spiegelstraat

Facing the courtyard to the rear, the Tolkien Suite is painted a deep, burnt tomato-red

Unusually for Amsterdam, some rooms are more the size of lofts: the Picasso Suite measures seventy square metres

This new hotel is in a double-fronted Empire house on Amsterdam's prestigious Prinsengracht

Breakfast in a hamper: a basket-full of delicious surprises is prepared for guests who cannot bear to leave their room

The stair hall revives the eighteenth-century tradition of the print room, with prints stuck directly onto the wall

Roman antiquities, African tribal art and the proprietor's own oil paintings sit on the mantelpiece of the salon fireplace

The Shakespeare Suite, a handsome, fifty-square-metre room, is elegantly decorated in tones of grey

The top-floor Picasso Suite has an elegantly high ceiling and five windows overlooking the canal

Seven One Seven is curtained and upholstered throughout in traditional men's suit fabrics

The Schubert Suite – a cosy, antique-filled room with shutters, an original beamed ceiling and a view of the canal

The Mahler Suite – English antique oak and African photographs make this the most popular room

Afternoon tea, included in the room price, is served in the library, a light-filled room stacked with design books

The Stravinsky Room is a private dining area overlooking the courtyard – dinner is served by prior arrangement

The quiet and secluded courtyard is an unusual but welcome rarity for a canal house in Amsterdam

The house number is also the name of the hotel, situated on the Prinsengracht – the Prince's Canal

The decoration is a personal, eclectic mix that throws together cast-iron urns and Murano glass

Luxurious angora-wool blankets were custom-made by the Melin Tregwynt mill in Wales; copper beds were sourced from Deptich Design in London; and architectural salvage dealers in Antwerp and Brussels supplied fireplace surrounds and other antiques. Anything that couldn't be found was commissioned from local craftsmen. Despite the rush, there was little compromise.

For Kees van der Valk it was the realization of a creative fantasy. As a graduate of the Rietveld Academy, one of Holland's top art schools, van der Valk started his career by diving enthusiastically into fashion – men's fashion. That was in the late sixties, the time of Pierre Cardin and Yves Saint Laurent, and anything was possible. Thirty years later, with the eye and attitude of a designer who has seen everything, it is perhaps not surprising that his own preference is now firmly rooted in the classic tradition of English bespoke tailoring, and so much so that the fabrics we normally associate with Savile Row – the pinstripes,

tweeds, hunting checks and houndstooth fabrics from such famous suppliers as Yorkshire-based Hunt & Winterbotham – have ended up as curtains and on chairs, couches and cushions in Seven One Seven. The wardrobe of a distinguished gentleman has become the wardrobe of a distinguished interior. Curtains are lined with raincoat fabric, partition curtains are made from Belgian twill (usually used for military uniforms), and even Suzannah, the resident Irish setter, sleeps in a basket upholstered in Harris tweed.

An impeccably turned out environment, Seven One Seven also has the very best calling card: an unbeatable location. Within easy strolling distance of the Rijksmuseum and the Van Gogh Museum, around the corner from the main antiquarian shopping street, Spiegelstraat, and within easy walking distance of all the best bars, restaurants and shops for which Amsterdam is justifiably famous, Seven One Seven is a perfect introduction to the sophisticated side of Amsterdam.

address Seven One Seven, Prinsengracht 717, 1017 Amsterdam, Netherlands

t +31 (20) 427 0717   **f** +31 (20) 423 07 17   **e** info@717hotel.nl

room rates from NLG 595

de witte lelie

Situated in the heart of Antwerp on the famous Keizerstraat, one of the city's oldest streets, this hotel has quite a pedigree. Dating back to the Flemish Golden Age, no less than three of the townhouses on the same street were once part of the life of Peter Paul Rubens. One belonged to his wealthy brother-in-law Balthazar the Great; another to Rubens' close friend, the mayor of Antwerp; and the third to another friend and colleague, the famous animal painter Frans Snyders.

This legacy of Antwerp's gilded past proved an irresistible drawcard to Monica Bock when she came across the opportunity to purchase three adjoining seventeenth-century townhouses in 1993. Inspired by all this history and charged with the idea of creating a small, intimate hotel, she and her interior designer sister, together with architect Bernard Coens, seized the challenge of combining a precious and prestigious heritage with the modernity they felt was crucial to comfort and convenience. The exclusive inner-city 'retreat' they envisaged had to be beautiful but it also had to be practical, with large bathrooms, efficient heating, up-to-date electricals, cable television and stereo – everything in fact that contemporary lifestyles demand. This meant difficult choices had to be made on what to take away and what to keep. Resisting the temptation to divide the accommodation into a warren of little rooms, Bock decided to do the opposite: create fewer but bigger rooms. There are just ten suites in the hotel, each completely different in configuration, but all luxuriously spacious and flooded with natural light. They therefore preserve the most powerful aspect of the original interior, namely the exquisite scale of its long rectangular rooms and soaring ceilings that typify the elegant proportions of the Golden Age.

As a result the interiors of De Witte Lelie are strangely reminiscent of the world depicted in the art of the period. Staying here, it feels as if you have wandered into a painting by Vermeer. There is a clarity to this hotel's style that allows simple little canvas-covered chairs to coexist comfortably with huge baroque chandeliers. Nothing at De Witte Lelie looks out of place and nothing feels forcibly fashionable.

Its sophisticated, timeless combination of antique and modern gives De Witte Lelie a very romantic ambience. This trait of course is what distinguishes the Flemish Belgians from their Low Country Dutch neighbours.

A grand staircase, black-and-white marble floor, and lofty ceilings create the ambience of an elegant classic

Canvas-covered modern furniture from Italy contrasts effectively with antique fireplaces and old beams

Breakfast at de Witte Lelie is served in the former stables, now an elegant room overlooking the courtyard

Adjoining the breakfast room
is a romantic all-white, old-world
kitchen, where breakfast is prepared

All the rooms at de Witte Lelie
are suites: elegant, spacious,
white and comfortable

The black-and-white floor of the
lobby recalls the houses portrayed
by Flemish Masters

The Belgians are more sensuous; they care more about food and less about train schedules; by and large they are more concerned with comfort and luxury than with exactitude. And yet this romantic streak is tempered with a strong sense of modernity. As anyone in touch with the worlds of fashion, interior design or architecture will tell you, the Belgians can be extremely avant garde. Just look at some of Antwerp's restaurants and shops. Many people come from Germany and Holland for the weekend not just for the food but also because Antwerp has some of the most original boutiques of any European city. (The staff at De Witte Lelie can make the best, and most up-to-date, recommendations for shopping and eating in Antwerp.)

Knowing the Belgian penchant for food, I thought it strange at first that De Witte Lelie does not have its own restaurant. But given its location in the very heart of Antwerp's old city, it would be a pity not to go out and sample some of the fine choices in dining that the city can offer. De Witte Lelie does, however, have a kitchen, and it's used to prepare the breakfast (included in the room rate). And what a breakfast it is. Served in what were once the stables, a charming, light-filled, lofty space overlooking the courtyard, the whole event is superbly orchestrated by the proprietor and manager, Monica Bock. She loves this part of her day, and it shows. The entire experience feels less like staying at a hotel than being a guest at an exquisite house party.

The entrance to the breakfast room is via the spectacular all-white kitchen (also straight out of a Vermeer painting) where the aroma of freshly brewed coffee and croissants just out of the oven is only a teaser for what awaits on the table. All manner of breads, pastries, cheeses, hams, sausage and home-made jams adorn the spotless white linen, and should you want some eggs, they are cooked to your exact wishes in the cast-iron pan that is brought to your table. Thus even breakfast resembles a still-life by a Flemish Master.

---

address De Witte Lelie, Keizerstraat 16–18, 2000 Antwerp, Belgium

t +32 (3) 226 19 66   **f** +32 (3) 234 00 19   **e** hotel@dewittelelie.be

room rates from 6,800 BF

the sukhothai

Sukhothai, or 'Dawn of Happiness', is regarded as the first true Thai kingdom. Established in 1238 in what is now north-central Thailand, it was a golden age of Thai art and civilization, a period of creativity and originality that exerted tremendous influence over subsequent periods. The kingdom itself was surprisingly short-lived, lasting only until 1376, when it became a vassal state to the city of Ayutthaya. But despite this brief lifespan it was the period of Thai history during which a national identity was forged. The Thai script was invented and Theravada Buddhism, the form practised in Thailand, was codified. It was also a period that saw the emergence of an art form – of which mainly architecture and sculpture survives – that is unique to Thailand.

In choosing the name Sukhothai, inspired by the achievements of that period of cultural flowering, this hotel gave itself a lot to live up to. Conscious of such a formidable precedent, a concentrated effort was made to evoke, in a modern sense, something of the harmony and beauty of this remote period of Thai history. To do this the hotel called on the talents of Edward Tuttle, the designer responsible for Phuket's famously idyllic retreat, the Amanpuri.

For his guiding inspiration Tuttle chose the tradition of the fabulous historic cities of Siam (as Thailand was always known before 1939). It is said that when the city of Ayutthaya was at its peak, it was one of the grandest and wealthiest cities in Asia – a thriving seaport envied not just by the Burmese but by Europeans too. The Portuguese were the first to arrive, in 1512, soon followed by the Dutch, Spanish, English and French, all of them by all accounts in great awe of the city. It was from this legacy that the Sukhothai hotel took its design cue. Set amid six acres of landscaped gardens and lily-choked reflecting pools, the sumptuous royal palaces of Siam's ancient capitals are evoked by the abundant presence of the sculpture, textures, colours and materials of Thai heritage. In the specially crafted brass lamp holders, the terracotta frames inserted into the plastered walls, the solid teak bathroom floors, the Thai silk upholstery, and particularly in the courtyard pond exhibiting replicas of thirteenth-century Sukhothai stupas, Tuttle has abstracted the most beautiful and distinctive aspects of Thai culture and reintroduced them in a manner that is elegantly pared down and unmistakably contemporary.

Tuttle's restrained teak, granite and silk have prompted some journalists to describe his design for the Sukhothai as 'Asian minimalism'. Though certainly not an inaccurate description, this still doesn't quite do the project justice. For the Sukhothai is more than an exercise in style: it is a successful attempt to project the best of Thai culture in a context where it can make a more memorable impact than in any museum. It involves the visitor to Bangkok in an extraordinarily old and refined culture which predates the Mediterranean Bronze Age by two thousand years. In fact the part of Southeast Asia we now know as Thailand was, according to world-renowned scholar Paul Benedict, the 'focal area' in the emergent cultural development of early man.

In contrast to Bangkok's recent transformation into a metropolis with some of the world's worst traffic, and in defiance of the city's conformity to the international trend for more and more high-rise towers, the Sukhothai consists of an enclave of buildings that vary in height from four to a maximum of nine storeys, all capped by simple pitched roofs. Located in the heart of Bangkok, a stone's throw from the exquisite Lumphini park, and in the centre of the lush and leafy banking and diplomatic sector, the hotel is a welcome haven from the frenetic activity of Asia's largest city. With four different restaurants (including the Celadon, one of the most authentic Thai restaurants in Bangkok, set in a traditional Thai pavilion in a water garden), six acres of flower gardens and lily ponds, a twenty-five-metre surface-tension swimming pool (its water continually spilling over the edges), a shopping arcade, beauty salon and doctor's clinic, there is no need for the jaded traveller to venture out at all. No wonder that the Sukhothai was voted the best hotel in Bangkok by *Business Traveller Magazine Asia* for three consecutive years.

In an age when we are often too rushed to absorb local colour, the design of the Sukhothai treats guests to the best of more than 750 years of Thai art and architecture.

address The Sukhothai, 13/3 South Sathorn Road, Bangkok 10120, Thailand

t +66 (2) 287 02 22 **f** +66 (2) 287 49 80 **e** info@sukhothai.com

room rates from US $250

hotel arts

In the years leading up to the 1992 Olympics the entire city of Barcelona looked like a building site. If it didn't exist (a stadium or an airport, for example) it was built, and if it was looking run-down (like most of Gaudí's architectural legacy) it was renovated. Emergence from years of isolation under the iron-fisted authoritarian regime of Franco had unleashed a passion to catch up, and huge investments were being made in technology and particularly in design. The city was undergoing a massive facelift and the architects and designers responsible became the city's new celebrities. It used to be said that Barcelona was a working city, like Milan – no one would consider coming here for fun. But times have definitely changed. Things are happening here and people want to come and see for themselves. The Olympics were the spark that ignited a full-blown renaissance. A lifestyle renaissance. People now talk of *nuevo* Barcelona, and Hotel Arts may well be its most potent symbol.

There are certainly few references to Barcelona's past in the architecture of this imposing monolith designed by US architects Skidmore, Owings & Merrill. The tallest building in Barcelona, it is distinguished by a gleaming white metal framework, a scaffold-like skeleton of immense proportions that envelops the entire tower. Structurally, this protects the building from tremors and strong winds; visually, it is like a beacon that draws people to the recently rediscovered beach. Reclaimed from swamp land, the area surrounding the Hotel Arts, including the new marina, is now starting to mature into a seaside playground and yet another side to Barcelona's multi-faceted personality.

It used to be said that Barcelona lived with its back to the sea, and in pre-Olympic days it did so for good reason: the coastline was no more than a collection of derelict wharves heaped with vacant, half-dilapidated port buildings and dirty sites of heavy industry. Now the old sea wall has a far more glamorous role: it divides a four-kilometre stretch of raked sand into two public promenades packed with cafés and thronged with café society. Being next to the beach is without doubt one of the biggest attractions of Hotel Arts. Away from the traffic, noise and crowds of the city centre, adjacent to the marina, on the beach and yet still in the heart of the metropolis (ten minutes by cab), this is a hotel where you can get out of the city without having to leave it.

The lobby, furnished with pieces by Barcelona designer Pete Sans, sets the contemporary mood of the hotel

While most of this duplex suite is bright and white, the bedroom was created in sombre shades of navy blue

It seems almost impossible to build in Barcelona without reference to Gaudí, and Hotel Arts is no exception

The spectacular duplex corner apartments were originally to be sold, but are now part of the hotel

The winter garden, a light-filled lofty space, is perfect for coffee on a winter morning

Its external skeleton of white-painted steel makes Hotel Arts a distinctive Barcelona landmark

White cotton upholstery and the warmth of honey-coloured timber distinguish Tresserra's 'Casa Blanca' chair

Designed by Skidmore, Owings & Merrill, the tower's grid absorbs the energy of strong winds and tremors

The light-filled duplex apartments facing the sea were designed and furnished by Jaume Tresserra

The large windows allow an
uninterrupted view of the
sea from the bed

The tapas bar, Boyescas, features the
quixotic furniture of famed Barcelona
architect Oscar Tusquets

High-tech architecture combines
with water-filled courtyards to lend
a contemporary yet Spanish flavour

Duplex apartments on the hotel's
top floors must be the world's most
architecturally dramatic hotel rooms

Navy blue leather pieces by Jaume
Tresserra, white linens and the dark
parquet floor of a duplex bedroom

A massive fish sculpture by US architect
Frank Gehry fronts Barcelona's tallest
building and defines the beach front

Tapas, the Spanish custom of nibbling
with a drink, is the perfect introduction
to Spanish cuisine

The all-marble bathrooms are open-
plan, allowing spectacular views of
the city or ocean from the bath

Overlooking a water-filled internal
courtyard, the fitness centre
takes up two floors

In an area that less than a decade ago was marshland, people now play beach volleyball, eat in beachside cafés, stroll around the massive marina complex admiring all the swanky yachts, and generally indulge in a seaside experience that, in Franco's day, was only to be had by driving out of the city and either heading north to the Costa Brava or south to the Costa del Sol.

In addition to the distinctly hedonistic attraction of its location, the towering size of Hotel Arts also introduces the benefit of scale. Rising a majestic 153 metres above the sea, the hotel offers 455 rooms and extraordinary facilities. This is the first European property for the Ritz Carlton group, and they didn't skimp on anything. There is a large, beautiful swimming pool with its own private deck overlooking the sea, a two-storey gym of a size more often found in Manhattan than Europe, and of course spectacular views over the Mediterranean, the marina and the city from most rooms. Yet despite all the mod cons there is never any mistaking that you are in Barcelona. Throughout the hotel, furniture by some of Spain's most gifted designers is featured alongside a substantial collection of contemporary Spanish art (hence the hotel's name) including artists Miguel Rasero, Xavier Grau and Mateo Vilagrasa. The hotel's tapas bar Goyescas, for example, features the highly distinctive furniture of architect Oscar Tusquets, a one-time collaborator and protégé of Salvador Dalí. As a result, the atmosphere could not be more evocative of Barcelona. By investing in art, architecture and design, the Ritz Carlton group has created a distinctive style and ambience. No wonder *Tatler* magazine voted it hotel of the year in 1997.

People still compare Barcelona to Milan – because it is still an important industrial centre – but with its new-found *joie de vivre*, they also now compare it to Naples. Perhaps this is why, despite its size, the Hotel Arts is almost always booked to capacity. Everyone, it seems, would rather be by the beach.

address Hotel Arts, Carrer de la Marina 19–21, 08005 Barcelona, Spain

t +34 (93) 221 1000 **f** +34 (93) 221 1070 **e** rc.barcelona.reservations.manager@ritzcarlton.com

room rates from 50,000 ptas

bleibtreu

A young hotel on an old street, Bleibtreu is a streetwise hangout behind the gentlemanly guise of a city townhouse. Situated on Bleibtreu Strasse, a famous little stretch of expensive boutiques just off the Ku'damm (the Kurfürstendamm, Berlin's great shopping boulevard), it's a welcome addition. Now, finally, the chic shoppers of Berlin have somewhere to go for lunch or a quick cappuccino. The only problem is that no one, taxi drivers included, seems to know that this is a hotel. Admittedly it's a brilliant disguise. From the street the Bleibtreu is a deli, a café and a flower shop, with a bar (the Blue Bar) and a restaurant (the 31) directly behind the café. The hotel part of the equation is subtle, very subtle. Between the café and the trendy florist there is an archway over a diagonal path leading into a blue-pebbled courtyard. Situated beneath a beautiful old chestnut tree, the courtyard looks out over the restaurant and then leads back inside to a small desk tucked into a corner. This is the front desk, the reception desk … in fact the only desk.

In deciding to be different, Bleibtreu has blown away all hotel conventions, including the lobby and the reception desk. Why waste space, they say, on chairs that people never sit in and tables that spend most of the day supporting fresh flower arrangements? They have a point. Why waste the space when it can be used for fun things like cafés, bars, delis and restaurants? This way the hotel becomes a real part of the city, a participant in everyday life. And for the guests it makes a refreshing change. Instead of asking the concierge (which they don't have anyway) for suggestions on the city's latest and greatest, you can simply hang out here, secure in the knowledge that you're not missing out, because this is the place where it's all happening.

But it's not just in the public spaces that Bleibtreu has decided to be different. The rooms also follow a new spirit perhaps best described as an eco-based design logic. A desire for calm and healthy well-being underpins both the fine detail and the overall concept of this hotel. Special organic porous paints allow the walls to breathe, all carpets are one hundred per cent virgin wool and the furniture is of untreated oak. Toxic chemicals are as much pared down as the interior aesthetic. But does that mean the place looks like a collection of hospital rooms? Far from it. The overall impression created by this eco-friendly approach is a kind of soft, new-age modernism.

Natural timber, natural colour
and organic paint express Bleibtreu's
eco-sensitive approach to design

Each floor of Berlin's Hotel Bleibtreu
is colour-coded: yellow and white
define the second floor

Timney-Fowler's neoclassically
inspired fabrics are combined
with fifties furniture

With a manager who used to be
a chef, food is taken very seriously
at Hotel Bleibtreu

An off-the-wall wall-clock is the
only decoration in the ground-floor
reception area

The Blue Bar is a popular little
pre-dinner haunt adjacent to
the ground-floor café

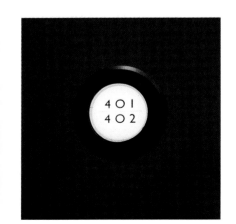

Even room numbers are done
differently – as illuminated
portholes set into the wall

Cotton sheets, hypo-allergenic wool
carpet, linen and cotton upholstery, and
an apple instead of a chocolate

Dressed in the style of a neoclassical
tented pavilion, the top-floor rooms
make the most of attic spaces

The delicatessen (along with a café and a flower shop) is one of the unconventional lobby tenants

The crisp, shiny terrazzo floors of the stair hall are made of glass chunks set in polished cement

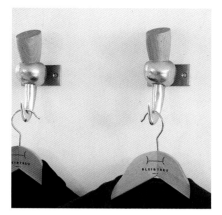

Modern, organic, funky, different: this is how best to describe Bleibtreu

Each floor has a different colour scheme: the top floor is black, white and red

The café, where guests and locals drop in for a quick cappuccino and croissant, has great ambience

The ground-floor flower shop is as much an attraction for locals as for hotel guests

Taking up most of the ground floor, the restaurant has a view over two different courtyards

Some of the sun-drenched top-floor rooms facing Bleibtreu Strasse feature small terraces

The ground-floor courtyard makes the hotel entrance an unusual outdoor-indoor-outdoor experience

It reminds me, for some reason, of California – of the interior of a 'fifties' beach house on the Pacific coast. The rooms are bright, clear and gentle, with nothing aggressive about them, nothing hard-edged. Being here inspires you to eat fruit and practise yoga … and then ruin it all by misbehaving in the bar and restaurant downstairs.

All of the accessories, furniture, carpets and lamps were specially designed for Bleibtreu by Herbert Jakob Weinand and made by hand in Germany and Italy. But perhaps the most unusual and attractive feature of the design is the lighting – and not just the lamps themselves but the manner in which they are controlled. All the lights – bedside, ceiling halogens, bathroom, make-up mirror and ambient – can be not only dimmed, but dimmed independently of each other. Once the desired mood is reached, they can be set and the levels recorded. All the adjustment and programming is done with a special remote control which (thankfully) the staff explain how to use. Press a button and the lighting level you prefer is recalled from memory. Now that's what I call a smart room.

Even the gym did not escape Weinand's comprehensive vision. In fact it's not a gym, it's a 'wellness centre'. This is not a place where you exert yourself, but a place where other people exert themselves to help you, the guest, relax. The greatest effort required of you is that of opening the door to the sparkling steam room and lowering yourself into the dipping pool. Situated in the basement of the building, the spa space is one of the most beautiful I've seen. There is also a massage centre with a full-time holistic masseur and, most intriguingly, a special post-steam relaxing area that uses coloured lighting to help stimulate a particular mood (red light for people going out, blue light for those having an early night). If it all sounds very different, that's because it is.

And what, ultimately, is the point of all this eco-friendly concern for your well-being? The answer is elementary – a good night's sleep.

address Bleibtreu, Bleibtreustrasse 31–10707 Berlin, Germany

t +49 (30) 884 74 0 **f** +49 (30) 884 74 444 **e** info@bleibtreu.com

room rates from DM 276

the ritz-carlton
schlosshotel

Even the bathroom slippers feature the insignia 'Designed by Karl Lagerfeld'. It appears on everything from the matches to the complimentary bathroom cosmetics. The point that the Ritz-Carlton Schlosshotel is making is that this is no ordinary hotel. And clearly it isn't. Even without the input of Germany's most famous name in fashion, this palace, in the exclusive Grunewald area of Berlin, would be impressive enough. Originally built for Walter von Pannwitz, an aristocratic lawyer with a passion for Meissen porcelain, law reform and Dutch Masters, it was, from the day it was completed in 1914, one of the most extraordinary residences in Berlin. Kaiser Wilhelm II was entertained here on a regular basis throughout the war, as were many of Europe's reigning royals. Berlin in the early twentieth century was the fastest growing and most vibrant capital not just of recently unified Germany but of all of Europe, and Palace Pannwitz quickly became the most exclusive address in Grunewald, the city's finest neighbourhood.

Grunewald (literally 'green forest') was an area developed from the royal hunting forests that surrounded the old Prussian city. Careful planning (including the creation of a series of lakes) and strict zoning that permitted only one house per two hectares of land ensured that Grunewald, intended as an exclusive residential area, would stay that way. And it has. Conveniently located at the beginning of the Kurfürstendamm, Berlin's super sophisticated shopping strip, Grunewald today is still a forest. As Karl Lagerfeld exclaims in the hotel video, 'where else in the world can you stay in a palace, in a forest, in the middle of the city?'

The German recession following the devastation of World War I brought an end to the high life in Grunewald, and the Pannwitz family, despite having built the house as the ultimate expression of their passion for art, architecture and design, were forced to follow Kaiser Wilhelm into exile in Holland. The house was never a home again. Schloss Pannwitz remained closed and shuttered for the better part of a decade and after wartime use (first as the Croatian embassy and then as British Army HQ) it was finally converted to a hotel during Germany's Reconstruction period.

Today, because of Lagerfeld's involvement, the old palace is probably closer to its original design than at any time since World War I. Rather than impress upon it his personal stamp, Lagerfeld chose to defer to history.

Kaiser Wilhelm II was a frequent guest in the days when the Ritz-Carlton Schlosshotel was a private villa

The Kaiser Suite has all the sumptuous grandeur of a Prussian prince's boudoir

Suitably formal and impossibly grand, the Vivaldi restaurant offers one of the finest dining experiences in Berlin

A chic lobby where guests can sit down when they check in – how civilized!

Karl Lagerfeld's own suite is in the cultivated and affluent Geheimrat architectural style

Lagerfeld's suite, available if he is not in residence, features the work of avant-garde French designer André Dubreuil

A team of talented craftsmen from Poland was brought in to restore the gilded panelling, the massive doors and the ornate detailing that originally embellished the grand spaces of Herr von Pannwitz's house. Other craftsmen set about the task of renovating the hotel's numerous paintings and its substantial collection of antiques. The result speaks for itself. The Ritz-Carlton Schlosshotel offers not just the opportunity to stay in a palace in a forest in the city, but also an opportunity to experience a style and architecture that these days only exists in coffee-table books and heritage houses. Where else can you dine in a room originally designed to entertain a Kaiser and a Tsar? Or lunch in a winter garden intended for afternoon teas with the Dutch and Danish royal families? But part of the fun is the fact that all this happens right in the centre of the city, meaning you can indulge in a sumptuous lunch, a stroll through the forest, and some serious shopping … all in the same afternoon.

Lagerfeld, however, did get an opportunity to put his personal stamp on one part of the hotel. In consideration of his involvement he was given an apartment within the old palace – the original private apartment in fact of Walter von Pannwitz. This was his opportunity to impart an individual signature. The suite, comprising a small entrance hall, a generously proportioned sitting room with views of the garden, and an equally large bedroom, was redecorated in a style that is rich without being fussy; elegant, but not too dainty or refined. Lagerfeld created this style by introducing select antiques and works by his favourite avant-garde designer André Dubreuil and the architect Borek Sipek. When the apartment is not in use (which, owing to his schedule, and all his other houses, is most of the year) it's available for hotel guests as an alternative to the other suites. Just for the bathroom alone it's probably worth it, not to mention the cachet of being able to say 'oh yes, we just spent the weekend in Karl's place in Berlin'.

address The Ritz-Carlton Schlosshotel, Brahmsstrasse 10, 14193 Berlin, Germany

t +49 (30) 895 840   f +49 (30) 895 84801   e ritzcarltonbln@aol.com

room rates from DM 465

hotel im wasserturm

A decade ago, Andrée Putman was the most sought-after designer in the world. The style that she created for herself in a loft space in Paris was the catalyst for a seemingly never-ending series of prestigious design commissions.

Spare, elegant and unmistakably French, the sense of style Putman introduced was one prevalent in Paris just before World War II. It is very similar in spirit to the work of legendary designer Jean-Michel Frank. Svelte, disciplined and entirely free of frippery – no knick knacks, no cushions, no frilly fabrics, no chintz curtains – Putman's creations were not so much design as a visual extension of who she was. Design and designer were one and the same. She was already well known to an inner circle of Paris cognoscenti, but after completing the design of Morgan's Hotel in Manhattan she became an international star.

Nobody had seen anything like it. The rooms followed Putman's pared-down preference, rooted in the concept that 'modernity is best glimpsed through dramatic understatement'. The bathrooms, for example, adventurously tiled in black and white with self-standing, unadorned stainless-steel sinks, were among the most photographed spaces of the early eighties. New York had its first cool hotel. Instead of catering to people's tastes, people had to adjust their tastes to the hotel. And it worked. Morgan's enjoyed among the highest occupancy rates in New York and for Putman it was the stepping stone to bigger and better things. She launched her own furniture company, Ecart International, manufacturing lamps originally designed by Venetian legend Mariano Fortuny and furniture by then-forgotten architect Eileen Gray, and she was commissioned to work on a uniquely innovative and daring architectural metamorphosis: the conversion of a nineteenth-century water tower, the largest of its kind in Europe, into a luxury hotel.

This was a dream job. Not only was the tower round – her favourite shape – but the sheer scale of the building promised extraordinary proportions. And there was the plus that the consortium commissioning the hotel had a reputation for insisting on quality. Where perhaps a lot of her work in New York was compromised by budget restraint (maximum effect for minimum cash) this consortium took a typically German long-term view and went for quality. The doorknobs, the furniture, the lighting, the fabrics, the bathrooms: every carefully considered aesthetic hotel im wasserturm

detail came off the drawing boards of her design company. The result, completed in 1990, is one of the most original and refined hotel design experiences in Europe.

And for once, the best rooms are not the most expensive. Situated on the sixth floor, these studio rooms are reached via a high-tech steel bridge suspended within the hollow core of this gigantic brick structure. The space, entered through imposingly tall doors of African Wenge wood, is divided into two rooms: a living area/study and a bedroom with en suite bathroom. With impossibly high ceilings and a pristine white tiled floor, it's the kind of space I would love to have as an apartment. It's all anyone would need, a splendid lesson in the importance of scale and space (quality) versus size (quantity). With their round walls, elegantly tall windows and timeless velvet-upholstered furniture inspired by Putman's trademark love of the thirties, these rooms are an inspiration for the potential of space given the right approach.

Anyone with an eye for interior design and architecture could lose themselves for hours in the extraordinary attention to detail. But there's more. Especially in the summer months the Wasserturm also happens to be one of Cologne's most popular restaurants. Situated on the roof and built (inevitably) in the round, this glass-enclosed space, with its myriad of sliding doors, opens out on to a terrace with a panoramic vista of Cologne. The view takes in the famous cathedral, the Rhine and the old medieval city built alongside. Here Putman abandoned her pared-down signature and recreated instead the style of a typical bourgeois Parisian restaurant, complete with comfortable reproduction Louis XV chairs, large round tables and crisp linen tablecloths. This struck me as an odd design choice given her penchant for spareness and simplicity. But then I remembered an interview in which Putman was asked her definition of good taste. She replied that she distrusted perfection – 'I always look for the mistake'.

address Hotel im Wasserturm, Kaygasse 2, 50676 Cologne, Germany
t +49 (221) 2008 0   **f** +49 (221) 2008 888   **e** info@hotel-im-wasserturm.de
room rates from DM 320

52

the manor

Shahjahanabad ain't what it used to be. Very little remains in modern-day Delhi of the city built by the powerful Mughal ruler Shah Jahan. Whereas the monument to his wife the Taj Mahal remains beautifully intact, the city from which he ruled what in its day was the most splendid, opulent and culturally advanced of all the Islamic empires has all but disappeared.

When the Muslims from the north invaded the Hindu principalities of Rajasthan, the resulting blend of cultures produced a society that excelled in art, architecture and mathematics to a degree that was the envy of the rest of the world. With an extraordinarily high level of learning and a plentiful population to do the work, the successive rulers of the Mughal empire built great palaces and massively fortified cities. They adopted the traditional Rajasthani technique of building in stone covered by a layer of finely polished lime render, and erected gleaming monuments to their massive power and wealth. Of all the Mughal rulers, none was more prolific or extravagant than Shah Jahan. The strength and wealth of his empire allowed him to embark on the all-white, all-marble folly of the Taj Mahal, and if his death hadn't thwarted him, he would have built its twin in black marble on the other

side of the Jumna River. But what of his seat of power, Shahjahanabad? Why does so little remain of the Mughal splendour of the city now known as Delhi? The answer is simple: a couple of centuries of modernity. The British followed the Mughal example and made Delhi their base. They soon began reshaping it according to their vision of what a city should be. As an imperial capital, they reasoned, it should have good transport connections to other regions of India. This was the great age of rail, and the iron road was given priority over ancient city walls. Following the model of London, different stations were constructed to service different destinations. The old city walls were breached in so many locations that it was hardly worth preserving what was left.

The next big change was ushered in by the next big transport revolution. An entire new city plan was proposed in order to accommodate the motor car. Sir Edwin Lutyens, an acclaimed British architect with royal connections, was given the task of designing a whole new city on a site just to the south. Like Haussmann's Paris, New Delhi was to be a city of broad boulevards and imposing buildings, monuments, grand parks and plenty of open space.

Luxurious but not plush: silks, dark wood and soft lighting distinguish the unfussy, distinctly linear guest rooms

Bold horizontal planes executed in crisp clean white are the hallmark of the Manor's 1950s architecture

Breakfast is served on an immaculate terrace overlooking the hotel's private croquet lawn

Italian craftsmen were brought over to lay the exquisite terrazzo floor, detailed with rectangles of Indian marble

Tactile, textural modernism: the property is protected by a massive sliding gate of intertwined bronze strips

Delhi is now the most congested city in Asia, but the Manor is a verdant haven of unexpected peace and quiet

Though it certainly wasn't part of the original plan, New Delhi was eminently well-suited to become the capital of independent India in 1947. Nehru himself was keen to build a modern India. He was instrumental in recruiting Le Corbusier to design the government buildings of Chandigarh, and encouraged foreign embassies to be bold and adventurous in the design of their buildings. Delhi soon became India's most modern city.

All this explains how a hunting lodge came to be built in the pure, streamlined style of the 1950s. The building has survived well, even if the radiating urban expansion of Delhi has wiped out all trace of the forests where the lodge residents once hunted. The Manor is a case of the right idea in the right place at the right time. Ten years ago there were still more bicycles in Delhi than cars; today this Asian city claims the dubious distinction of the heaviest traffic in the East, more even than Bangkok. But as a major city, Delhi has come into its own. The 1999 opening of this creatively contemporary hotel was one more confirmation of Delhi's new cosmopolitan credentials. For visiting traditionalists set on maharaja-style palace experiences, the Manor might come as quite a shock. This eighteen-room hotel is a showpiece of 1950s horizontal concrete construction. The interior by Vinay Kapoor and Shirley Fujikawa of London-based Studio u+a opts for a pared-down, almost minimal approach that allows the rich palette of natural materials to do the decorative talking. Bathrooms clad in green granite, walls surfaced in gold leaf, panelling in warmly hued woods, and a floor of Italian terrazzo inlaid with small squares of Indian marble exemplify the subtlety and appropriateness of the design. The experience of staying here is equally relaxed, calm and soothing. Tucked away in a leafy street in the exclusive New Friends Colony, the sprinkler is the loudest noise you are likely to hear. Indian materials, textures and finishes executed in the International Style: totally unexpected, totally Indian.

address The Manor, 77 Friends Colony (West), New Delhi 110065, India
t +91 (11) 692 5151 **f** +91 (11) 692 2299 **e** manordel@vsnl.com
room rates from US $155

the clarence

The Clarence is not a new hotel. It has been part of the Dublin scene since 1852, when it was first built as a railway hotel for out-of-towners. Located in the heart of Dublin's Temple Bar district, on the banks of the River Liffey, the hotel, by virtue of its architectural integrity and its prime location, has always managed to retain dignity and charm, even when it was well beyond its prime. It was this faded charm that endeared the hotel to the artists, musicians and writers who began to make Temple Bar the happening area in Dublin in the seventies. Among the regulars enjoying a pint at the Clarence in those days were members of the band U2. Fond memories of the place prompted Bono and the Edge to join a consortium of Irish investors to purchase the hotel with a view to restoring it.

As one American journalist observed, 'rock stars used to trash hotels, now they own them'. But of course rock stars, if anyone, should know a thing or two about hotels, since they live in them for months on end when on tour. The Clarence renovation, accordingly, was determined to a great extent by U2's own vision of their ideal place to stay. They wanted an intimate hotel, with great service, in the tradition of Irish hospitality, yet not stuffy and

definitely contemporary in its design direction. To realize their vision they employed some of the best people in the industry. Paris-based Grace Leo-Andrieu, advising manager of Hôtel Montalembert and proprietor of the recently renovated Hôtel Lancaster (also Hip Hotels), was brought in as consultant, and Keith Hobbs (a former associate of Terence Conran) of London-based United Designers was given responsibility for design.

And design is what sets the Clarence apart. In the early 1900s the hotel was renovated in the Arts and Crafts style, with distinctive sober panelling in Irish oak, practical leather chairs and the occasional flourish of terrazzo floors. This 'oak and leather' came to distinguish the Clarence in the memories of several generations of regulars, and it was therefore decided that the Arts and Crafts style should also form the basis of the new interior. Hence the new Clarence is defined from top to toe, from the public spaces to the forty-nine guest rooms, by a subtle palette of Portland stone and American oak, and by the rich colours (cardinal red, royal blue and gold) of its leather-upholstered chairs, sofas and benches. *Condé Nast Traveler* magazine described its interiors as 'understated – in a context of unstinting luxury'.

The Tea Room, the Clarence's award-winning restaurant, features traditional Irish dishes with a continental twist

The 'Study', in the Arts and Crafts style, is a quiet and relaxed place to enjoy a continental breakfast or evening drink

A substantial collection of original works by Irish artist Guggi is dispersed throughout the hotel

The Clarence's all-white tiled bathrooms continue the Arts and Crafts style of the ground floor

The lobby is a warm and inviting place with original Irish oak panelling installed at the turn of the century

Rooms are calm and comfortable, with Egyptian cotton sheets, solid oak furniture and white Portland stone

It's a style that makes the Clarence a very comfortable place to stay, yet without making it too precious. As Harry Crosbie, one of the founding entrepreneurs, explains: 'the hotel couldn't be too rarefied – Dubliners wouldn't stand for it'.

Comforts aside, the real drawcard of the Clarence is Dublin, and the best place to start to get to know this city is the hotel's very own Octagon Bar. At night the Octagon fills up with its eclectic mix of residents and eccentric locals. As Crosbie tells it, 'the brilliant part is that the Clarence has always been part of the Dublin scene and, now that we've redone it, it's still part of Dublin' – which is a polite way of saying that he is really happy they didn't mess it up. This they certainly didn't do. On weekends the bonus of being a hotel guest is that you'll actually get in. Many, many people don't. Hefty guys are stationed on the Liffey, as well as the Temple Bar entrance, to stop the stampede. Even in Ireland, it seems, there's a limit to how many people it takes to make a happy bar.

Then there's the restaurant. The Tea Room, the most talked-about restaurant in Dublin, is situated in the hotel's impressive former ballroom. Huge windows flood this double-height space with natural light. Under the direction of chef Antony Ely, the Tea Room serves a surprisingly affordable contemporary cuisine specializing in Irish classics with a continental twist such as grilled fillet of new season lamb with celeriac purée and black olive jus.

For guests eager to get out of the hotel and explore the city of Dublin, this is the perfect location. The Clarence is smack in the middle of Temple Bar, a neighbourhood that serves up a heady mix of urban sophistication and grass-roots Irish ambience. Return sober from a night out in this area and there's something wrong. And the night life is only half the story. During the day, if you can resist the temptation to stay in nursing a sore head, go and check out one of the best-preserved Georgian cities in the world.

---

address The Clarence, 6–8 Wellington Quay, Dublin 2, Ireland

t +353 (1) 407 0800 **f** +353 (1) 407 0820 **e** reservations@theclarence.ie

room rates from IR £210

the peninsula

The Peninsula is *the* Hong Kong hotel. There are newer hotels, and there are hotels that offer more luxuries (though I'm not sure what they could possibly be), but none could encapsulate the total Hong Kong experience the way the Peninsula does. This is one of very few hotels in the world that are both grand *and* hip. The minute a hotel is described as grand usually marks the beginning of the end: too many navy blue blazers and too many readers of the *Robb Report* rapidly transform grand into old-fashioned, snobby and pretentious. The Peninsula has avoided this fate by staying ahead of the times. It may be one of the oldest hotels in Hong Kong, but in terms of attitude it's one of the youngest. On the very top of the towering building is the very hip China Clipper lounge bar designed by Denton Corker Marshall for guests departing by helicopter. One floor down, with a spectacular view over the neon drama that is Hong Kong harbour, is the Philippe Starck-designed Felix restaurant, a firm favourite with Hong Kong's designer-black crowd, and one of the most photographed restaurants in the world. Its food – a mix of Pacific ingredients and styles – is every bit as adventurous as Starck's design. Twenty-eight floors down is the 1920s-inspired

restaurant Spring Moon. Here the look is dark, decadent and colonial, and the food is refined Cantonese.

Despite all the modernity, the 'Pen' is an institution. In a city with little affection for nostalgia, and where very few colonial relics have been preserved, the Peninsula is the big exception – a building that is representative of Hong Kong's past as well as its present. The history of Hong Kong itself can be traced through the history of this hotel. Architects were first commissioned to draw up plans for 'the finest hotel east of the Suez' back in the early 1920s. The Pen was the first to cater to the overland trade (in the days when a first-class train trip from London took ten days, running via Calais, Paris, Moscow, Beijing and Shanghai); first to entertain the stars of Hollywood in the thirties (Charlie Chaplin and Paulette Goddard); and first to open a disco in the sixties. In the seventies the Pen assembled the world's largest fleet of Rolls-Royces to transport guests from the airport in style.

Like many Hip Hotels, the Peninsula is a family business. It all started with two brothers of Jewish-Iraqi descent. Ellis Kadoorie settled in Shanghai in 1880, while his elder brother Elly set himself up in business in Hong Kong.

Unparalleled views of the glowing neon spectacle of Hong Kong by night are one of the Peninsula's greatest attractions

Witty detail is Philippe Starck's design signature: these miniature pharaonic staffs are salt and pepper shakers

The twenty-seventh-floor men's room is a decadently theatrical space with one of the best views in all Hong Kong

A rather grand, neoclassically inspired pool is in a massive space half-way up the building

The China Clipper bar is the ultimate departure lounge, located directly below the hotel's own helipad

Felix, the double-storey restaurant on the twenty-seventh floor, designed by Philippe Starck, is consistently popular

PHILIPS

Over the next two decades the Kadoorie brothers made their fortunes, achieving success in banking, rubber plantations, electric power utilities and real estate, and gaining a major share-holding in Hong Kong Hotels Limited. By the time Sir Ellis was knighted in 1917 (he was also a generous patron of charities, another family tradition) Hong Kong Hotels Ltd's prestigious properties included the Peak and the Repulse Bay Hotels in Hong Kong; the Astor House, the Palace Hotel and the Majestic in Shanghai; and the Grand Hotel Wagons Lits in Beijing.

The Peninsula, the jewel in the family crown, was completed in 1928. Twelve years later the baton passed to the next generation when Lawrence (later Lord) Kadoorie, son of Sir Elly, became chairman of the board, to be replaced in 1946 by his brother Horace. With the loss of the Shanghai properties to the government of the People's Republic of China in 1949, the Peninsula became the unchallenged flagship of the company.

By the time three thousand revellers gathered in 1988 to celebrate the Pen's sixtieth birthday, the grand old lady was showing her age. It fell to the latest Kadoorie, the Hon. Michael D. Kadoorie, to bring this venerable establishment into the twenty-first century. His response was a daring scheme to add a thirty-storey tower to the original structure. This was to house another 130 guest rooms, plus a heliport, the Felix restaurant and a spectacular swimming pool and spa designed by Orlando Diaz-Azcuy.

In the process, the Peninsula managed to keep the elements that made it great and get rid of the stuff that made it stuffy. Luckily they still send a Rolls-Royce to pick you up at the airport, the soaring lobby is still the place for a traditional afternoon tea and the service remains beyond impeccable. You no longer need to be in a suit for dinner – unless it's a black one, of course. As the *Asian Wall Street Journal* astutely noted, 'what attracts the clientele is the clientele.'

---

address The Peninsula, Salisbury Road, Kowloon, Hong Kong

t +852 2920 2888 **f** +852 2722 4170 **e** pen@peninsula.com

room rates from HK $3,000

great eastern hotel

Welcome to the sandwich-shop centre of the western world! Until recently, the City of London offered little to match the lifestyle and urban sophistication for which the capital as a whole has earned a reputation.

The City is London's commercial heartland, a great world centre of the legal, banking and insurance industries, but it has always been a bit of a wasteland in terms of the finer things in life. Each lunchtime, hoards of grey-suited clones briefly escape their large corporate containers, to return only minutes later with sandwich bag and newspaper to be devoured one on top of the other. Working in the City has always struck me as an awfully big price to pay for getting rich. Then along came Sir Terence Conran. In the late 1990s he acquired the grand Victorian railway hotel directly behind Liverpool Street Station and brought to it his West End magic. The result is a kind of contemporary lifestyle centre, not so different from the hugely successful Bibendum and Bluebird – only bigger. Much bigger.

Great Eastern is a giant. Besides the 267 bedrooms and suites – all different – the complex contains five restaurants and at least three bars (four if you include the exclusive members-only club). It's as if Conran decided to make up for every one of the City's shortcomings in one all-inclusive venue. The teaming mass of grey suits now needs look no further than the Great Eastern for Japanese sushi, British roast beef, or the latest fusion cuisine. And judging by the lunchtime crowds, most have decided to do exactly that. Residents of Chelsea, enamoured by the seafood of Bibendum's oyster bar, now have a weekday equivalent in Great Eastern's Fishmarket Restaurant. Fans of sushi and other Japanese fare can opt to dine in the slick contemporary interior of Miyabi, while enthusiasts of the more traditional British pub can get a (warm) beer and roast dinner in the Tudoresque surroundings of the George Bar. For more formal occasions or working lunches (which seem to have become much more popular since Great Eastern opened its doors), there is the Aurora Restaurant, a grand old space complete with leaded glass, a dome cupola and snooty waiters. Underneath huge modernist chandeliers constructed of overlapping flaps of paper, diners enjoy a menu that's billed as modern European cooking at its best. It's a spectacularly beautiful space that unfortunately is not as extraordinary as it would be if only it were populated by a few more women.

Rooms at the Great Eastern get larger as they get closer to the ground. Whatever the size, no two are the same

The George is the hotel's traditional English pub, serving British ale and modern versions of classic pub food

Guest rooms come in two styles: dark timber and rich colour (nocturnal luxe) or white and blond (for morning types)

Relief-patterned plaster and a feature wall of polished timber in the reception recall the glory days of rail travel

This grand Victorian railway hotel was built to accommodate travellers arriving at Liverpool Street Station next door

Fishmarket is the City's answer to Bibendum's Oyster Bar in the West End, also a Conran project

But there's no such gender disparity in Terminus, the modern all-day brasserie that has clearly become the preferred option to the soggy sandwich on the desk.

Most of these drinkers and diners, I'm sure, are pretty oblivious to the fact that one can also stay at Great Eastern. But many visitors to London do need to be in the City, and this is truly the first place to offer a survivable option. The visitor has advantages over the day guest, not least of which is the use of the substantial fitness centre. Tai chi, yoga, weight training, cardiovascular conditioning – the list of options is as varied as the hotel's list of restaurants and bars. The fact that the gym complex is set in a grand Victorian room designed in the manner of an Egyptian temple doesn't hurt either.

Variety seems to be the dominant theme at Great Eastern. Stylistically, guest rooms range from dark, dense and sophisticated to light, bright and blond. They become progressively grander and larger as they get closer to the ground floor – a fairly novel arrangement for a hotel. Large or small, dark or light, they all share contemporary design details like Frette linen sheets, Jacobsen work lamps and Eames desk chairs. But the real plus, particularly for overseas visitors, is the hotel's splendid heritage. Liverpool Street Station, opened in 1875, was one of the great temples to the age of steam. When work began on the adjacent hotel shortly afterwards, provision was made for it to have its own tracks and sidings, not just for the convenience of the guests but also for bringing in sea water for the hotel's sea baths. Travel then was for the very privileged, and the hotel architecture reflects the extravagant demands of its elite clientele. Corridors had to be wide enough for cabin trunks, and features such as the glass dome and main staircase had to be stupendously grand. In the process of renovation, these historic features were carefully preserved as modernity was intelligently inserted. With Great Eastern Hotel, Conran has really proved that you can breathe new life into a grand old girl.

address Great Eastern Hotel, Liverpool Street, London EC2M 7QN, UK

t +44 (20) 7618 5000 **f** +44 (20) 7618 5001 **e** reservations@great-eastern-hotel.co.uk

room rates from £210

one aldwych

Underwater Mozart – nothing more vividly captures the extra attention to detail that separates One Aldwych from other five-star luxury hotels. Music in the pool, television while you shave, an in-house cinema for private screenings, fibre-optic lighting, politically-correct vacuum plumbing that uses 75 per cent less water than conventional systems: Gordon Campbell-Gray has created a unique hotel by considering details beyond the conventional – details that even grand hotels would consider extravagant.

Inspired by the Montalembert in Paris and the Aman chain in the East, Campbell-Gray – a veteran hotelier whose previous project was the very successful Maidstone Arms in East Hampton, Long Island – was convinced that there was room in London for a more contemporary approach to being spoiled. His experiences in the playground of the rich and famous, where his neighbours included Calvin Klein and Martha Stewart, had taught him a thing or two about the dreams and demands of the modern luxury customer. At One Aldwych Campbell-Gray took the Montalembert's approach and added a luxury checklist of his own. In design, he was intent upon eliminating the chintz and paring down the plush –

clearing out the claustrophobic clutter that has traditionally defined luxury. This is why, at One Aldwych, the walls are white, the fabrics are plain and the decorative detail is limited to the odd bolt of colour in the rich tones of Jim Thompson Thai silk. There's not a tassel in sight. This is not to say that the rooms or the lobby lack warmth, however; ambience is provided by lighting and by the collection of contemporary art, both of which have been given an appropriate degree of emphasis.

Campbell-Gray was very clear about the kind of hotel One Aldwych was to be – comprehensively modern but not so avant-garde or trendy that you could quickly tire of it. It was to be practical rather than fashionable. Thus each room is equipped with American as well as European modem plugs (ISDN) to accommodate the ubiquitous laptop of the working traveller. And despite London's inflated property prices, the rooms are sized to contemporary scale, ie generously spacious. The service too had to be immaculate. 'The greatest indulgence for me when I am travelling,' says Campbell-Gray, 'is to stay in my room, watch a film and order room service. A hotel has to be able to do a great hamburger no matter how acclaimed the restaurant might be.'

WOODHAMS

The aim was to eliminate 'the dripping deluxeness' – to banish any hint of snobbery and instead contribute something of value to the guest experience. That is why the hotel recruited leading personal trainer Matt Roberts to manage the immaculate fitness centre, with its glamorous Bugatti blue mosaic tiled pool. And that is why Campbell-Grey hired ex-Ritz Julian Jenkins as the executive chef for the mezzanine restaurant Indigo. There is also the more formal dining option of Axis, a dramatic double-height space with a 1920s feel, distinguished by a massive mural by English artist Richard Walker and accessed by a spectacular flight of travertine stairs. And the guest who has had enough of elaborate restaurants and fusion cuisine is catered for by the very streetwise Cinnamon Bar – a more svelte and European version of New York's Dean & Deluca deli.

All the details and services that have been pumped into this hotel make it one of the world's most accommodatingly luxurious places to stay. Even so, its most impressive element remains the architecture. This classically elegant corner building, originally built in 1907 as the offices of the Morning Post, is one of the most important Edwardian buildings in London. Its dignified Louis XVI-style stone exterior bears more than a passing resemblance to the Ritz – which makes sense given than it was designed by the same architects, Mewès and Davis, the Anglo-French partnership that was also responsible for the Paris Ritz.

Last but not least is One Aldwych's location. What still sets London apart from all other world cities is its vibrant theatre scene. In this respect, no hotel is better located. Most major venues, including the South Bank Centre, Shakespeare's Globe, and the Royal Opera House, are within walking distance.

An architecture of gravitas, cutting-edge technology, understated elegance, polished service, culinary choice, superb location – all these conspire to affirm Oscar Wilde's famous quip: 'living well is the best revenge'.

address One Aldwych, London WC2B 4RH, UK

t +44 (20) 7300 1000 **f** +44 (20) 7300 1001 **e** sales@onealdwych.co.uk

room rates from £250

the hempel

Who among us is not fascinated by the Zen notion that to achieve serenity and contentment we must jettison the baggage we schlepp around in daily life? We clutter our lives with scores of meaningless possessions. They become a burden and soon we are enslaved to them. Without any possessions – or at least with just the bare minimum – we can once again be free to enjoy ourselves and our lives.

It sounds a reasonable proposition, and could even be true, but only the very, very brave among us would take everything we own to the tip in order to test it out. A more sensible option is to check into the Hempel, for here is a hotel where you can sample 'minimalism'. The Hempel is named after London-based design dynamo Anouska Hempel, who first made her name in the world of Hip Hotels with her other London creation, Blakes. To create the Hempel she set up her own team of architects (AH Designs) and worked side by side with them for three exhausting years. The result is a hotel that is cool, white and empty on a monumental scale, a place of Zen-like simplicity. Set behind a row of five perfectly restored Edwardian townhouses in the previously overlooked but now up-and-coming area of Bayswater, just north of Hyde Park, it is the embodiment of Anouska Hempel's belief that space is the ultimate luxury in a big city.

Yet while the Hempel welcomes guests with its acres of white space, it is certainly not a cold or clinical environment. The lobby, described by *Harpers & Queen* as 'larger than an Olympic size swimming pool', is entirely paved in oversize squares of classic Portland limestone and distinguished by a series of geometric cutout spaces that admit pools of warm sunlight. At night, it glows with light and warmth from two very long, very low and very 'horizontal' hearths that must rank as the most elegant fireplaces of any hotel in the world.

The whole interior was conceived according to an oriental concept of simplicity. 'For ten years I've wanted to create this kind of hotel', explains Hempel. 'It's the result of a desire for radical change.' The design is based on a marriage of occidental and oriental. Eastern influences are reflected in the collection of mahogany umbrella stands from Bombay, artfully arranged along one vast lobby wall, in the Indian bullock carts that serve as occasional tables in the uninterrupted symmetry of the sunken lounge, or in the eighty-one potted orchids that define the entrance room.

Tucked into a corner of the Hempel lobby, the library is a space for quiet contemplation

The food at I-Thai mixes Italian, Thai and Japanese cuisine; the presentation is equally exotic

The lobby is a soothingly geometrical, almost temple-like space tiled in acres of limestone

Mahogany umbrella stands from Bombay and a chair by Australian designer Marc Newson

The fresh and innovative bathrooms have been featured extensively in fashion and interiors magazines

Hidden behind a towering screen of sand-blasted glass, I-Thai's bar is a quiet little cocoon of a space

The fusion of East and West is above all evident in the extraordinary hotel restaurant, I-Thai. Presided over by a chef formerly of the Oriental Hotel in Bangkok, I-Thai serves a creative mix of Italian, Thai and Japanese cuisine in dishes such as sea bass in rice paper served with a pesto risottini. This cuisine is presented in a fashion perhaps best described as 'edible architectural maquettes' – sculptural arrangements so intricately composed that you start your meal with a certain tinge of regret. But I-Thai is not purely a case of cleverly sculptural *théâtre végétal*, the seventeenth-century art of arranging still lifes to be painted by a master such as Rubens, Van Dyck or Rembrandt. The quality of the food easily matches the standard of the presentation: it's every bit as delicious as it looks.

Even the hotel's garden continues the pared-down theme. Situated in a traditional square opposite the entrance it is almost as if every leaf has been styled to Anouska Hempel's exacting standards. Individual teak and brass recliners – the kind that used to be found on old ocean liners – are positioned between ornamental trees and herb-filled borders. Three square pools echo and reflect the formal architecture of the hotel facade. Particularly in summer, the lavender- and rosemary-scented garden adds another dimension to the hotel.

Anouska Hempel has been described as bordering on the fanatical in her attention to detail at this hotel. That may be true, but as a guest you can only be the beneficiary of her inability to compromise. One room has a floating bed, suspended in the middle of the room like a giant cage; others have a stone bath built into the window recess; in some bathrooms the tap water is illuminated at night by fibre optics. The success of the Hempel emphasizes one glaring truth about minimalism: the more you leave out the better what is left has to be. It is not for the faint-hearted. Less *is* more – more demanding and more exciting.

address The Hempel, 31–35 Craven Hill Gardens, London W2 3EA, UK

t +44 (20) 7298 9000 **f** +44 (20) 7402 4666 **e** hotel@the-hempel.co.uk

room rates from UK £235

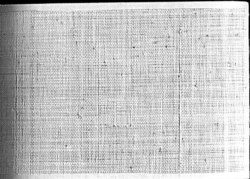

westbourne hotel

Notting Hill is London's equivalent of SoHo, New York. It's the neighbourhood with the most interesting shops, some of the best bars, and – as most residents like to think – the most interesting people. It's as representative of today's London as Chelsea was of the swinging sixties. Long before the film came out, Notting Hill had morphed into the most fashionable place to live in London. Twenty years ago it was a different story. It had potential, but mainly because property was so cheap. Its old Edwardian boxes in the neoclassical Georgian style are arranged in stately fashion along elegantly curving tree-lined streets. The area was a renovator's and bargain-hunter's paradise, and it inevitably attracted the crowd with more imagination than cash. The raw, real style of the area was a plus, as was the local market on Portobello Road, which has since grown into an institution. Today, Westbourne Grove and Ladbroke Grove still show glimpses of the originality and wit that first brought a renaissance to this area. Unlike most other high streets of London, you will not find the same old chain shops here: no French Connection, no Body Shop, no Boots the Chemist. Instead the place is punctuated with genuine boutiques – one-off shops like Solange Azagury (jewelry),

Nick Ashley (utilitarian menswear) and Space (state-of-the-art furniture). On the food front, instead of a Sainsbury's or a corner shop you'll find Tom's Deli, a delicatessen-café that disguises itself as a deceptively downmarket grocery store but where a table for Saturday morning brunch is a hard-won prize.

To launch a hotel right in the middle of this hyper-hip area is obviously a smart move – but also one fraught with risk. Expectations are high, and to fail to live up to the area's style reputation would be a disaster. Westbourne Hotel is located in a house typical of the area, and it's not clear what to expect from the outside. The proprietors – young financier Benjamin Fry, club impresario Orlando Campbell and project coordinator Giles Baker – decided against minimalism or faux glamour. Instead they chose a mid-century modern look. The interiors are modern but not overbearingly so – they are also rich, sensual and tactile. The handwaxed leather furniture is bound to evoke a few 'hey we used to have a couch like that before my mother gave it to the church'-type comments. But ultimately it's not the individual pieces that distinguish this place so much as the way the different ingredients have been combined – especially the art.

Works by some of the hottest names on the British art scene are to be found in the lobby, restaurant, corridors and guestrooms. The displays were put together in collaboration with London gallery Sadie Coles. Some of the art is witty, some peculiar, some so obtuse as to be a private joke – but never is it safe or boring. There is a fascinating selection, including Allison Jackson's photograph of Dodi and Di, Keith Coventry's *Bronze Kebab*, even a framed pair of Union Jack Y-fronts by Abigail Sallis. Established talents like Bridget Riley and Craigie Aitchison are displayed alongside Britart stars Gavin Turk and Sarah Lucas (who designed the cigarette wallpaper).

Each guest room is different, but they are unified by a palette of exotic timber veneers set against white walls. The interiors are neither far out and funky nor predictable and boring. The aesthetic is like the area – different but not outrageously so. In fact the hotel reminds me of the best boutiques in Notting Hill: clean simple spaces where you can find unusual, unexpected pieces. Westbourne Hotel whispers originality, it doesn't yell it from a distance.

The London press was recently less than kind to Benjamin Fry after he dared to suggest that the Groucho Club, Soho's notorious celebrity hangout, could do with an update (his update). What a yuppie upstart, they fumed. What would someone who has never crashed under the billiard table or witnessed Damien Hirst putting his willy in a plate of scrambled eggs know about running a club? The assumption was that he would ruin the Groucho by designing it to pristine perfection. One look at Westbourne Hotel tells you that's exactly what would *not* happen. Westbourne is not perfect. It's not a design statement. It isn't even particularly pace-setting – and that's the point. It combines a look that wouldn't be out of place in the pages of *Wallpaper* with the slightly shabby, 'let's not try too hard' style of Notting Hill. Someone like Damien Hirst could be quite comfortable here – with or without his willy on a plate.

---

address Westbourne Hotel, 165 Westbourne Grove, Notting Hill, London W11 2RS, UK

telephone +44 (20) 7243 6008   **fax** +44 (20) 7229 7201   **e** wh@zoohotels.com

room rates from £175

the portobello hotel

The Portobello doesn't feel like a hotel. It feels more like spending a few days with a rich, funky aunt who happens to live in London's Notting Hill.

For the past three decades the Portobello Hotel has been a true original in a world of overwhelmingly bland hotels. In a way it is the granddaddy of Hip Hotels – the original eccentric outsider that kick-started the current trend for small, offbeat hotels where the interior design is cutting-edge, staff are attentive but discreet, and lobby and rooms alike are intended to feel as intimate as home. This is a nesting experience without the drudgery of tidying up. Established in 1971 by Johnny Ekperigin and designed by Julie Hodges, the Portobello has consistently been one of London's most desirable places to stay.

As *Newsweek* magazine recently pointed out, 'the Portobello discovered long ago that the key to success was to play up its quirks and style'. This is a hotel that happily flaunts its own eccentricity. The rooms – unusual, inventive, cosy and very sexy – have that much admired haphazard, casual look that is deemed to be so typically English. This unlikely mishmash of styles attracts an equally unlikely mishmash of legendary guests: like the ageing rocker Alice Cooper, who requested regular deliveries of white mice from the local pet shop to feed the boa constrictor that he kept in the bath; or Tina Turner, who fell so much in love with the place that she just had to buy the house next door.

Some of the Portobello's rooms have become as legendary as the guests themselves. Take the room with 'the waterworks', for example, a hippy-style suite equipped with what can only be described as a 'Victorian bathing machine': a marvellously eccentric collection of copper pipes, taps and a massive sprinkler, all surgically attached to a turn-of-the-century claw-footed bath. This is a remarkable enough piece in its own right, but picture it standing in the middle of the room on its own little island of black-and-white marble tiles, directly behind a massive round bed tucked into the bay window, and you begin to grasp why this room has become so famous. Then there is the 'four-poster room', which contains an Elizabethan bed so high and large that you need a ladder to climb into it (honest). A canopy painted with clouds reinforces the giddy scale. And for those who like to hide in attics there are two fully-fledged Moroccan chambers tucked under the roof.

The vivid colours of a Turkish kilim used as a curtain set the sensuous ethnic tone of the Portobello Hotel

Moroccan chandeliers, Victorian antiques, muslin drapes, velvet curtains – this is eclectic, rock-star chic

A round bed set in a bay window overlooking a private park is the focal point of one of the most popular rooms

Victorian baths complement the
moody oriental atmosphere in
the Moroccan-inspired attics

The four-poster room features a gigantic
Elizabethan bed complete with oak
steps to enable you to climb in

Seashells embedded in a small
grotto: the view from the lower-
ground-floor restaurant

Moody, dark and dangerously seductive, their rich reds and layers of carpets and cushions evoke the atmosphere of a Berber tent.

Unlike most establishments that cater to the elite, the Portobello Hotel recognizes that 'elite' does not necessarily mean rich. So in a democratic spirit, it also includes rooms that are realistically affordable. Single rooms (somewhat ominously referred to as 'cabins', admittedly) do not exactly spoil the guest with space, but the design and decor is no less inventive. Equipped with an extravagantly tented campaign bed, they look like the kind of place Napoleon might have bedded down for the night. The less romantically inclined might be tempted to dismiss a Portobello cabin as nothing more than a tent bed in a closet; but what do definitions matter when you're staying in the middle of London's hippest neighbourhood?

This is the heart of Notting Hill, home to Europe's biggest annual street carnival. At the Portobello Hotel you are only a few paces away from the hectic hustle of the famed Portobello antiques market and the exceptionally cool shopping scene of Westbourne Grove, lined with some of London's most innovative and famous boutiques, not to mention bars, clubs, cafés and restaurants. Whether it's antiques and vintage clothing you are after, or just groceries and people-watching, Notting Hill is a treasure-trove and a parade. It is also a hot spot for the adventurous gourmand. London's cuisine has changed beyond all recognition since the days when a kebab or a quick curry were the most likely (probably the only) choices after a night out at the local pub. This city, Europe's largest, now leads the world in sophisticated and inventive cuisine, and Notting Hill has more than its share of reputation makers. As in all major cities, the place to be changes constantly (if not quite as frequently as New York), so the staff at the Portobello Hotel are the best bet for a local update on the latest and greatest.

address The Portobello Hotel, 22 Stanley Gardens, London W11 2NG, UK

t +44 (20) 7727 2777 **f** +44 (20) 7792 9641 **e** info@portobello-hotel.co.uk

room rates from UK £140

chateau marmont

Chateau Marmont is a legend. Think of a name, any famous name, from the world of showbiz – past or present, film, music or television – and there's certain to be a Chateau Marmont anecdote, scandal or connection.

This, after all, is where Paul Newman met his wife Joanne Woodward; where Jean Harlow carried on a scandalous affair with Clark Gable while still on honeymoon with cameraman Harold Rosson; where director Billy Wilder offered to sleep in a bath rather than suffer the indignity of staying elsewhere; where Jim Morrison of the Doors, high as a kite, jumped off the roof of a poolside cabana; where tough guy Robert Mitchum was photographed doing the dishes in an apron; and where John Belushi tragically died of a heroin and cocaine overdose.

Chateau Marmont on Sunset Boulevard has been an enduring feature of the Hollywood scene since the early thirties. Unlike the Garden of Allah, the Trocadero, the Mocambo, Schwab's drugstore and all the other star-studded hangouts that sadly no longer exist on Sunset, Chateau Marmont is still around. Ask a member of the older Hollywood set about the Marmont and their eyes will twinkle as if talking about a naughty but likeable uncle who once scandalized (and secretly delighted) the family with his outrageous exploits.

But there is a pitfall to being such a legend – the risk of getting stuck in a time warp. Not so Chateau Marmont. It has changed enough to remain current, but not enough to lose what it once had. This tricky balancing act between preservation and renovation is the notable achievement of New-York-based nightclub, hotel and restaurant impresario André Balazs. On buying the legendary LA property in 1991, Balazs was keenly aware of the prosaic reality that a hotel must update and improve or run the risk of attracting an increasingly diminishing circle of clients. That, in commercial terms, would be a certain death spiral. Yet he also faced pressure from a group of hard-core fans (including the likes of photographer Helmut Newton) to lose nothing of what the hotel had.

Thus, keeping in mind the advice of devoted regulars, the decision was made to upgrade, albeit in a manner that it was hoped would be hardly noticeable. This was no easy task. André Balazs rejected three separate schemes before settling finally on the combined talents of interior designer Fernando Santangelo and production designer Shawn Hausman.

Lamps at Chateau Marmont reflect the
theatrical flair of interior designer
Fernando Santangelo

The lobby is a popular hang-out
for actors summoned to the hotel
for a script reading

A fountainhead in the courtyard
of a building modelled after the
Château Amboise on the Loire

The generous proportions of the rooms
reveal the building's original intended
use as upmarket Hollywood apartments

Impossible to label, the salon's interior
is timelessly appropriate to the lofty
dimensions of its beamed space

Bathrooms, wherever possible, are
a carefully restored version of
the thirties originals

Black-and-white pictures in the 'thirties'
phone booths are a reminder of the
hotel's legendary history

The funky forties furniture, found by
production designer Shawn Hausman,
preserves the old Hollywood ambience

Despite being on Sunset Boulevard,
Chateau Marmont is blessed with
views of green from all sides

The vaguely forties ambience of the newly renovated suites is perfectly appropriate to the hotel's vintage

The restaurant is a ludicrously intimate place that seats no more than twenty and serves French-Californian food

The colonnaded private courtyard is a popular spot for breakfast, a quiet coffee or a late afternoon drink

The salon, in contrast to the guest rooms, is purposefully dark, moody and gothic

Embroidered Frette linen hints at the luxurious attention to detail: there is more to this hotel than reputation

The gym, a recent addition, is hidden away in the spacious, air-conditioned attic

In contrast to the dark and moody lobby the rooms are bright and white, furnished in a *faux* forties style

Gothic shapes and a time-worn patina mix well with most guests' preference for basic designer black

Gothic, gothic, gothic – despite Chateau Marmont's laid-back image, the attention to detail is anything but

Their contribution, exactly as Balazs requested, was to make the Marmont look as you would imagine it has always looked. Design was used to create an illusion (appropriately enough for a Hollywood hotel): the illusion that it has always been so. And it has worked … without skipping a beat. Regulars still wouldn't dream of staying anywhere else (enjoying, no doubt, the added extras of room service, not an option in the old Marmont, and an efficient telephone system, unlike the infamous 'pot luck' exchange of the past). And new clientele are attracted by the forties-style glamour of the rooms and the undimmed reputation.

The fact that Chateau Marmont was never intended to be a hotel is probably what makes it such an attractive one. Built in the twenties as an earthquake-proof imitation of the royal Château Amboise on the Loire in France (its foundations are on solid rock), the layout and size of the rooms at the Marmont owe their generous proportions to the simple fact that they were originally designed as apartments.

Perhaps this also explains why some guests check in for months at a time. Robert de Niro lived in the penthouse for two years, and Keanu Reeves doesn't even own a place in LA, preferring instead the comfort of the Marmont. One of the more recent famous names to make the Chateau Marmont a long-term West Coast habit was writer Dominick Dunne, who stayed there for the entire duration of the O.J. Simpson trial, which he covered for *Vanity Fair*.

In the best Hollywood tradition, Chateau Marmont is the kind of place where you can avoid leaving your room for weeks on end and no one will think anything of it. Room service, as might therefore be expected, does a roaring trade in this hotel. In fact so few guests venture out that the lobby, terrace and dining room are hardly ever too crowded − a very pleasant bonus for the odd guest *not* interested in locking him or herself away. Whatever it is that Chateau Marmont has going for it, one thing is certain: this is one Hollywood legend that doesn't disappoint in real life.

address Chateau Marmont, 8221 Sunset Boulevard, Hollywood, California 90046, USA

t +1 (323) 656 1010   **f** +1 (323) 655 5311   **e** chateaula@aol.com

room rates from US $275

mondrian

The Mondrian is very LA – it's big, it's glamorous, it's pretentious and it's filled with stars. This, the fourth hotel collaboration between Ian Schrager and his star designer Philippe Starck, truly captures the 'top down, sunglasses on' spirit of Los Angeles.

Located up on Sunset (where else?), looking across all of LA, the Mondrian is almost a cliché of the quintessential LA experience. First there is the pool: not especially large, it is true, more for dipping than swimming, but thanks to the extensive deck surrounding it and the quirky manner it has been furnished, an extremely popular place to hang out. It feels more like an outdoor lobby. The whole poolside experience is *Melrose Place* with more space, better design, and more inspiring dialogue. All you need are sunglasses, a sarong and your room key (how else can you show that yes, you are actually staying here, not just hanging out by the pool like so many of the other beautiful people?). The waitresses look good in their sarongs, and so do the chairs – for even the furniture follows the laid-back dress code. Who else but Philippe Starck would consider wicker wing chairs draped with brightly coloured sarongs as poolside furniture?

By and large the attitude at the Mondrian is 'see and be seen'. But if you're not in the mood to be ogled while having lunch, Coco Pazzo, the Mondrian's restaurant, provides privacy in a very Starck fashion by hiding tables behind a disciplined row of eight-foot-high flower pots – Godzilla-size versions of your typical kitsch terracotta pots planted with bay trees that provide welcome shade. At night, if the urge to be seen strikes again, the Mondrian has the hottest bar in town, the Sky Bar. Built in a style best described as a cross between an Adirondack rowing shack and a Bali beach club, this quirky outdoor pavilion is the place to be. If you can get in, that is. If you're a local and you ain't a star – good luck! One of the distinct benefits of being a guest is that you get to hang out and do some serious mingling in a place that normally wouldn't admit you. Just make sure you keep hold of that room key.

Bizarre but entertaining, the scene at the Mondrian is thoroughly LA. Any time it gets too much, the rooms are the perfect retreat. Vast, immaculate, all-white spaces (bar a touch of green and a light-grey carpet) they have a certain 'poolside cabana' feel – more like a Malibu apartment than a hotel room.

The Mondrian has instigated a trend whereby many pieces in the rooms are for sale, including the potted orchid

In the lobby bar, bowls of fresh fruit are topped up all day to encourage a healthy LA way of life

The terracotta pot is a recurrent design theme and a welcome change from inane beach umbrellas

Rooms are bright and big, with a full kitchen and breakfast space as well as a living area

This, believe it or not, is the concierge's desk. If you have travel needs or plans just sit at the table

Although the pool is not particularly large, it offers spectacular views over Los Angeles

The polished, modern environment of the lobby includes eccentric design anomalies, such as a huge log

Coco Pazzo, Mondrian's restaurant, is the West Coast twin of the New York restaurant of the same name

White is only right when, as here, the crisp bedlinen is perfectly ironed and immaculately clean

A deep-buttoned conversation corner tucked away in the lobby is vintage Starck

The lobby bar is locked away inside a mobile unit that opens at night to dispense cocktails

The Sky Bar, a separate outdoor pavilion overlooking the pool, is one of the hottest bars in LA

Adjacent to the pool deck, the gym has a free weights room, steam rooms and an assortment of running tracks

Starck's enormous terracotta pots on the outdoor deck are funny and practical, providing shade and privacy

Sari-covered wing chairs, Chinese ceramic stools, and old Bakelite phones are Mondrian's take on lobby furniture

Wicker wing chairs draped in brightly coloured sarongs: Mondrian's alternative to plastic banana chairs

The Mondrian's light-filled lobby bar is a popular place for a casual but stylish breakfast

The pool deck functions like a hotel bar – it's the place where people meet and hang out

Not only are they furnished with a kitchen and charming breakfast nook, but someone has already done the shopping. Stocked with enough provisions for a week, the mini-bar has been expanded into a mini-deli. In fact, the Mondrian takes the whole idea of the hotel doing the shopping for you to a new dimension. We've all seen the polite notices that invite us, if we really like the bathrobe, to *buy* one. The Mondrian invites you, if you really like the hotel, to buy the entire contents of your room. They provide a comprehensive catalogue, as detailed as a home insurance inventory, to help. Everything from the corkscrew to the potted orchid – chairs, plates, cushions, pencil cups, you name it – is listed and priced. Invited to a birthday lunch outside the hotel, I admit that the pretty orchid in a classic terracotta pot had the makings of a terrific present, and who would ever know that it was the result of the hotel's thoughtfulness rather than my own?

There's no question that the Mondrian is a hotel for sybarites. With its indoor–outdoor design chic expressed in a pale palette of white, biscuit and ecru, the Mondrian has a sensual quality that manages to merge the demands of the business traveller with the seduction of a resort. And just as well, because LA is one of those cities, along with Miami, Barcelona and Sydney, where the weather is a vital part of the experience guests demand of the hotel. Nobody would care if a hotel in London lacked a pool, but in LA it's important. It's these 'I'm here so spoil me' luxury touches that the Schrager-Starck team do so well.

Following a trend that Schrager himself started at the Royalton and the Paramount, the restaurant (Coco Pazzo), the bar (the Sky Bar), even the magazine and newspaper concession are all licensed to independent operators. This inventive bit of delegation ensures the hotel remains a fixture for a steady stream of local customers (who come for the food and ambience) as well as out-of-towners. Ultimately it's what makes the hotel, as Schrager would describe it, 'the nightclub of the nineties'.

address Mondrian, 8440 Sunset Boulevard, West Hollywood, California 90069, USA

t +1 (323) 650 8999   **f** +1 (323) 650 9241   **e** mondrian@travelbase.com

room rates from US $310

amanjena

Of all the Aman resorts in the world, this one had the longest build-up. For almost a decade the news that Marrakesh was to get an Aman intrigued travellers and locals alike. At times it seemed more like a rumour – a strategic bit of goodwill propaganda by Moroccan tourism officials, as if to say 'this city is now important enough to be the first and only place in Africa worthy of the very faithful and affluent Aman junkies'. No one knew where it was to be, much less what it would look like or what it would offer in terms of travel experience. There were sceptics aplenty. Sure, they argued, the Aman formula of microscopic attention to detail, aesthetic prowess and service honed to perfection is a winning combination in Asia – but then the culture of Asia has always been very strong on hospitality. Many doubted that Adrian Zeccha and his team could conjure the same kind of magic in an African Muslim state. The delay in opening only fuelled the negativity. See, critics said, they are delaying the whole thing on purpose because they know it's not going to work. The flow of adverse publicity was inevitably swelled by the departure of founder Zeccha from the group. It's a disaster, it's coming apart at the seams … the press was ready for the coup de grâce.

When it finally did open, Amanjena almost proved them right. People came away with stories of room service measured in hours not minutes, and the compound architecture was said not to live up to Aman's usual elevated standards. But if anything, the only mistake Amanjena made was to open too soon. If they had just waited a few months until the young but very enthusiastic staff had been properly trained, and until the newly planted palms had been allowed to mature a bit, it would have been obvious from the start that Amanjena is the best hotel in Marrakesh. Why? Let's begin with the architecture. Some critics have called Ed Tuttle's design monotone, sombre, lacking in vibrancy. I call it elegant, restrained and subtle. More importantly, it is in keeping with the design heritage of southern Morocco. Amanjena's forms echo those of Marrakesh's famous Menara gardens. The Arabic emphasis on water was a great influence. The buildings are arranged around a huge square reflecting basin on one side and along tiled avenues of fountains and pools on the other. Tuttle also captures the mystery of Morocco with a myriad of tall arched spaces that dissolve one into the next. Whereas La Mamounia – the Dorchester of Marrakesh – offers traditional Western hotel

architecture with a Moroccan twist, Amanjena's approach was to create Moroccan architecture toned down by a Western twist. All the elements are here – the mud texture, the arches, the hidden courtyards, the tiled roofs, the mosaic *zillij* – but they have been executed in a manner that values subtlety over impact. Black *tajine* earthenware dishes combined with black, green and beige mosaic offer a modern take on a traditional art form.

But it's not just authenticity and style that make Amanjena the best hotel in Marrakesh; there is also its unashamed devotion to luxury. Each guest is cocooned within a magnificent circular space complete with domed ceiling and fireplace. The en suite bathroom alone is the size of a Paris apartment, and each *maison* opens onto a private courtyard furnished as an outdoor living area in Moroccan style, complete with fountain and *minzah* or gazebo.

The entire setup is so stylishly seductive and luxuriously comfortable that it is tempting not to leave one's private compound. That would be a shame. Amanjena is minutes away from the medina of Marrakesh, one of the few intact medieval cities in the world. You should drag yourself away from Aman's hedonistic clutches and experience the intoxicating sights, smells and sounds of one of the most exotic cities on the planet. With streets and passages often no wider than two motorbikes or one fat donkey, the walled inner city of Marrakesh gives a taste of medieval urban life: exhilarating, cramped, dark, smelly, noisy, claustrophobic … in a word, fascinating. First-timers will be drawn to the vivid spectacle of Jemma al Fna, the vast open square at the gateway to the medina that features a daily circus of snake charmers, acrobats, pipe players, water vendors, and row upon row of market vendors. For shoppers, the souks of Marrakesh are alive with bargaining and deal-making over the ubiquitous glass of mint tea. And when the intensity of the Marrakesh experience all gets too much, you can retreat to the luxurious haven of Aman perfection.

address Amanjena, Route de Ouarzazate, km 12, Marrakesh, Morocco

telephone +212 (44) 403 353 **fax** +212 (44) 403 477 **e** amanjena@amanresorts.com

room rates from US $600

the adelphi

Pedestrians strolling through Flinders Lane, the heart of Melbourne's inner city, are liable to experience one of the most peculiar images imaginable if their gaze happens to travel skywards: the glimpse of swimmers doing laps eight storeys above the street. Perhaps stranger still is the view for the swimmers, gazing down at the roofs of taxis and trucks as they're about to make their tumble turns.

Needless to say, the Adelphi's one-of-a-kind cantilevered swimming pool has attracted its fair share of attention since the hotel first opened in 1992. But it would be an injustice to the hotel to dismiss this as nothing more than an attention-grabbing gimmick. In fact, the suspended glass-bottomed lap pool is an appropriate metaphor for the entire hotel: adventurous and unconventional. There is absolutely no aspect of the Adelphi – furnishing, detailing, design or otherwise – that shows any sign of compromise. This is a progressively minded, 'street smart' hotel that says, in design terms, 'if you don't like it, go somewhere else'.

A place as aggressively hip as this may come as a surprise to those unacquainted with Melbourne. This is a city of great cafés, good restaurants, trendy bars and architect-designed night clubs, and design plays a big role in these venues. Melbourne's art and architecture community is thriving, and it shows.

It helps, of course, in the case of the Adelphi, that the architects also happen to be the proprietors. Denton Corker Marshall, the Melbourne-based architectural partnership of John Denton, Bill Corker and Barrie Marshall, is one of the big architecture success stories in the East. With offices in Sydney, Jakarta, Hong Kong, London, Warsaw, Ho Chi Minh City and Tokyo, DCM are responsible for some of the biggest and most innovative architectural projects in Asia, including award-winning Australian embassies in Tokyo and Beijing. Yet despite their size, they are not corporate boys. They remain streetwise, with a passion for design that is reflected in this small project where they have truly put their money where their mouth is.

Playing the dual role of architect and client has allowed DCM not just to invent the space but also to determine the way it is furnished, and they went to considerable effort to translate their distinctive architectural signature into an interior design scheme. The guest rooms are elegant and spare with a black slab bed hovering over a black carpeted floor.

The deceptive achievement of DCM's design is to make the complex look remarkably simple

Only asymmetrical furniture designed by the architects themselves is permitted to interrupt the Zen simplicity of the space

'What's all the fuss?' asks architect Barrie Marshall, 'the pool only sticks out 1½ metres' (even if it is eight storeys up)

Only in a hotel owned, designed and operated by architects would you find pepper and salt mills by Ettore Sottsass

The bathrooms are as minimal as it gets, with polished Chinese granite floors and stainless-steel sinks

White bed linen, white Roman blinds: there is something inescapably sexy about such smooth simplicity

A view across the lap pool towards the Adelphi Roof Club, a members-only bar popular late at night

The restaurant interior is interrupted only by suspended photographs of architecture by John Gollings

The restaurant is all about polished concrete, intersecting angles and lots of white: an architect's space

The Adelphi's bedheads are simplicity itself, just sheets of ash-faced plywood, next to stainless-steel side tables

Intersecting planes of bright colour define the exterior and the glass-bottomed pool

Poolside on the roof is one of several places to hang out at the Adelphi, especially for sun-worshippers

The Adelphi café in the hotel's basement, where breakfast starts with the best caffe latte in town

The Adelphi is situated in Flinders Lane, home to Melbourne's top art dealers

The building's gutsy origin as an inner-city warehouse suited the architects' no-frills plans perfectly

An urban warehouse conversion is not what most people would expect of Melbourne

Even the restaurant chairs came off the drawing boards of Denton Corker Marshall, the architects and proprietors

A sandblasted glass partition wall with stainless-steel studs to hang a bathrobe from

Bedside tables are simple wedges of satin-polished stainless steel suspended from the wall, and the all-white walls are uninterrupted save by a single, abstract, angular piece of furniture in multicoloured leather. The bathrooms have even more of an edge. Floors of black Chinese granite paired with a long, sleek, stainless-steel slab, indented in the middle to form a sink-like trough, are pure simplicity, a Zen space to shower and shave.

Throughout the hotel there is not a single item, doorknobs included, that didn't come off the drawing boards of DCM. And the all-white café-restaurant downstairs and the black bar on the roof are like nothing you have seen before. The bar, only open at night, has the hotel's best view over Melbourne's metropolis, and the all-black interior – black rubber floor, black leather furniture and black-painted walls – only accentuates the view. In the basement, or rather the *souterrain* (for it still has windows to the street), the all-white interior of the café-restaurant, with its unique, custom-made

chairs of white nylon, is softened by the light grey of a bleached concrete floor, with the DCM trademark of brightly coloured metal bars dissecting the space.

The food, perhaps unexpectedly, is just as good as the design. The café-restaurant of the Adelphi is one of very few places in Melbourne to have been awarded three 'chefs hats' by *The Age*, the city's most respected newspaper (the equivalent to a Michelin star in Europe). This distinction has ensured that the place is full from eight in the morning until midnight.

On top of this, the Adelphi enjoys the best location in the city. Situated on the most avant-garde street in Melbourne (the address of all the major art galleries), it is around the corner from the major theatres and night clubs, and next door to the city's best shopping street, Bourke Street. The odd guest has been known to bang a shin against the stainless steel bedside table, but that's the only downside to all this uncompromising design. And surely it's better to be a little black and blue than to be bored.

address The Adelphi, 187 Flinders Lane, Melbourne, Victoria 3000, Australia

t +61 (3) 9650 7555   **f** +61 (3) 9650 2710   **e** info@adelphi.com.au

room rates from A$275

the prince

It all started with a pub – a classic Aussie pub on a corner of Fitzroy Street in Melbourne's seaside neighbourhood of St Kilda. Twenty years ago, this was a derelict and dangerous area. Like Miami's South Beach, St Kilda used to be the home of drunks and drug addicts, plus the occasional adventurous architect, irresistibly drawn to its rather grand Victorian architecture. Now St Kilda is like a beachside version of London's Notting Hill. It's chock-a-block with avant-garde boutiques, up-market delis, a plethora of cutting-edge places to eat, and a trendy clientele to match.

The last remaining stronghold of the former residents of St Kilda is their watering hole, the Prince of Wales. The Prince, as it is affectionately known, was a workers' pub. The front bar was a packed, heaving, aromatically challenged nightly scene, and no stranger to the odd fist fight. It was, as they say in Australia, 'rough as guts', a drinking hole straight out of the country's colourful folklore.

It was also a prime piece of urban real estate. Restaurant entrepreneurs John and Frank van Haandel knew the place well and they knew its potential. Just down the road, they had converted an old beach pavilion into Australia's most successful restaurant, the

Stokehouse. In acquiring the Prince, they realized a long-term ambition to take over the area's most substantial and infamous landmark. To the delight of the fiercely loyal locals, and to the surprise of everyone else, they started by doing very little. They didn't touch the front bar. But while the clientele were still spilling rambunctiously onto the street on big Friday nights, a building crew was quietly busy on the hotel's capacious upper floors, turning the seedy old accommodation into a collection of guest rooms more in keeping with area's new character. Exotic Thai silks, Danish design classics, the odd Australian sixties piece such as a Grant Featherstone chair, contemporary Italian furniture, and wicker lamps custom-made by local fisherman were artfully curated against the white walls of luxuriously spacious and light-flooded guest rooms. The brothers, both acutely design conscious, travelled the world to pick the eyes out of what the best hotels had to offer – and then improved on it.

Attractive as the rooms are, what most sets the Prince apart is the manner in which it has grown beyond the usual definition of a hotel. In a slow, almost organic process, the van Haandels have added one lifestyle venue after another to the old Prince of Wales pub.

the prince

First came Mink, an after-hours cocktail bar tucked into an unused back corner of the ground floor. For those who find the 'drink till you drop' culture of the front bar offputting, Mink offers a more ambient alternative in which to sample forty-three different varieties of vodka. Next came Circa restaurant, delicately designed in pink Thai silk and white leather. This has quickly forged a reputation as one of the best venues for Melbourne's signature fusion cuisine, a modern mix of Asian and continental influences – Thai, Vietnamese and Indonesian meet French and Italian. On the same floor, the restaurant was further embellished by the addition of Circ, a private dining room upholstered in wall-to-wall lime green deep-buttoned velvet, with an outdoor terrace shielded from the blazing Aussie sun by a series of suspended canvas sails. And on the first floor, with a nod to the view over Port Phillip Bay, a surfboard-shaped, moodily lit bar was opened for pre-dinner cocktails.

Most hoteliers would leave it at that, but for John and his brother Frank, this was still only the beginning. Next to the reception entrance they installed a bakery, complete with an old-fashioned delivery bicycle in homage to their father's bakery in the Victorian country town of Bendigo. This bakery, however, is also a café and it has become a popular spot for breakfast, particularly with trendy St Kilda residents on their way to work. The complex has also opened its own bottle shop for the odd person who might prefer to spend a night at home.

The hedonistic coup de grâce came relativity recently with the opening of the exclusive Aurora Spa Retreat. Its expansive space includes a magnificent indoor pool, yet another restaurant, and full spa facilities offering a wide menu of different indulgences.

Pale suites, Starck tubs, Vodka Mules, Danish design, bagels, brioche, mud packs – and a good old-fashioned Aussie pub. The Prince is a comprehensively cosmopolitan experience.

address The Prince, 2 Acland Street, St Kilda, Melbourne, Australia
t +61 (3) 9536 1111 **f** +61 (3) 9536 1100 **e** thedesk@theprince.com.au
room rates from A$190

138

marlin

The revamped Marlin mixes a funky futuristic style with splashes of Caribbean colour in a design that seems curiously reminiscent of the 1962 James Bond film *Doctor No*. And oddly enough, there is a connection. Ian Fleming, creator of James Bond, was the owner of a Jamaican estate called 'Goldeneye'. This estate was recently purchased by the founder of Island Records Chris Blackwell, who also happens to be the highly successful proprietor of a string of South Beach Hip Hotels, among them the Marlin.

In the film, Doctor No is the crazed scientist and master criminal who has built himself a mysterious island retreat in the Caribbean from where he intends to hold the world to ransom by threatening to unleash weapons of mass destruction. (No points for guessing who stops him.) But Doctor No is not just mad and evil; he is also extremely stylish. *Wallpaper* magazine would kill for a pad like his: a sexy combination of futuristic laboratory with acres of stainless steel, banks of computer screens (pretty advanced for 1962), thousands of flashing buttons, pared-down monochromatic furniture, streamlined grotto walls, and girls in silk kimonos continually disappearing behind big sliding doors.

The new Marlin Hotel could almost be Doctor No's Miami pied-à-terre. The shiny stainless steel has reappeared in the futuristic styling of the lobby; the computer screens have metamorphosed into giant television sets permanently tuned to MTV; and the guest rooms, with their built-in furniture, rounded walls and monochromatic colour scheme, resemble the organic grotto spaces of Doctor No's island hideaway. Alas, there are no smooth-sliding automatic doors, but Marlin guests *are* handed an armload of remote controls to operate the video, the stereo and the cutting-edge-technology web TV, which gives them internet access as well as an e-mail address.

The designer responsible for realizing this fantasy is herself a character straight out of a James Bond film. Permanently dressed in black, with silver hair and big black glasses, Barbara Hulanicki knows a thing or two about creating environments that attract a lot of attention. She was the name behind Biba, London's legendary but now defunct department store where the likes of David Bowie, Elton John and other glam rock stars once bought their silver platform shoes and pink Lurex T-shirts.

But it's not just design that makes the Marlin hip. A genuine effort has been made to define a new hotel experience. What good is it, for instance, to have a stereo in every room if there is nothing to play? Not a problem if the proprietor used to own a record label. A funky selection of brand new CDs sits next to each stereo (all available to buy should should you become too hooked) and each room throbs to a different beat. The noise? No problem. The rooms, as you would expect from a designer used to catering for rock stars, are amply soundproofed.

In fact the Marlin is very much a music hotel, with big-name musical guests in the past including U2 and Aerosmith. There are state-of-the-art fully equipped recording studios located at the far end of the lobby. Every night in the Marlin Bar is different, with visiting DJs spinning acid jazz, lounge, funk, hip hop, house and more. The scene in the bar is a regular nightly ritual which goes on until the early hours of the morning.

There's even a special reclining pit adjacent to the bar called the Shabeen Pillow lounge: a cosy, cave-like space, piled deep and high with hundreds of oversized cushions covered in colourful Caribbean fabrics. The ambience at the Marlin, as distinct from the frenetic salsa tempo of most of Ocean Drive, is best described as 'Cubarean': a spicy mix of hot Latin and cool Caribbean that defines the food as well as the music.

During the day the Marlin has the kind of unhurried, lazy attitude normally associated with the Caribbean islands. Just sitting in the lobby sipping a cappuccino can be entertainment enough. Johnny Casablanca's modelling agency Elite (the one that fired Naomi Campbell) is located on the second floor, so all day long picturesque persons, mostly on rollerblades, glide across the Marlin's original 1930s terrazzo floor on their way to yet another casting for a 'fun in the sun' photo shoot. No wonder Miami attracts the rich, the famous and the curious.

address Marlin, 1200 Collins Avenue, Miami Beach, FL 33139, USA

t +1 (305) 604 5063 **f** +1 (305) 673 9609 **e** reservations@islandoutpost.com

room rates from US $195

pelican

Miami is currently the fastest growing city in the US, South Beach is the fastest growing part of Miami, Ocean Drive is the fastest growing street in South Beach, and the Pelican is quite simply the 'fastest' hotel in town.

Nestled in among all the other candy-coloured, streamlined Art Deco hotels of Miami's Ocean Drive, the city's liveliest seaside strip, the Pelican is known as the kooky outsider. Owned and operated by Diesel, the Italian label that has made a mark with its satire on the pretences of the fashion world, this 1950s building in American 'motel' style has become the first expression in interior design of Diesel's unique and very hip sensibility: irreverent, slightly crazed, and fun.

If you really want to be in the thick of things it's impossible to be closer to the action. Next door is Lario's, Gloria Estefan's celebrated Cuban restaurant, two doors down is the News Café, *the* place to have breakfast, upstairs at the Pelican is the Miami chapter of the Ford modelling agency, and just across the street is the most popular stretch of the beach itself – the part with the volleyball nets, the rollerblading track, the never-ending parade of perfect bodies and a cameo role in every other American breakfast-cereal commercial.

Staying at the Pelican is like dressing up. You can be whoever you want to be in a room that dresses up with you. Feeling patriotic? The 'Born in the Stars and Stripes' room is for you. All hot from the music? Book the all-red 'Best Whorehouse' room. Feeling primitive? Try 'Me Tarzan, You Vain'. Spiritual? Spend the night in the 'Jesus Christ Megastar' room. Disco fever? The 'Psychedelicate Girl' room is definitely for you. And there are more – many more. Try 'Love, Peace and Leafforest', 'A Fortune in Aluminum', 'Some Like it Wet', 'Power Flower', 'Decocktail', 'Bang a Boomerang', 'Half-Way to Hollywood', 'Viva Las Vegas' or 'Big Bamboo'. Each and every one of Pelican's rooms is dedicated and designed to a theme. In design language this hotel is saying to you, the guest: 'This is a Latin city. Relax, enjoy yourself and give in to your imagination.'

Thankfully however, fantasy is not delivered at the expense of comfort. There is maid service twice a day, and every room is equipped with TV, video, quality stereo, fridge, and a minimum of two phones (one in the bathroom). Special examples of attention to detail include industrial ceiling fans and recycled oak floors (carpet in tropical Miami? No thank you.)

The 'Me Tarzan, You Vain' room
– a wild bit of Africa Graphica
on Ocean Drive

Bottle-cap baroque: the mirror is perfect
for the 'Executive Sixties' suite of
Miami's Pelican Hotel

Extravagant it may be, but the bathroom
of the madcap penthouse suite is believe
it or not its most sedate space

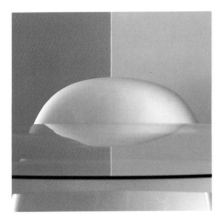

The 'Executive Sixties' suite with
a view of the beach is all colour
and fantastic plastic

'Best Whorehouse' – definitely
a blinds-down, lights-out
kind of a room

Designer Magnus Ehrland collected
what must be the world's greatest
hoard of garage-sale kitsch

The Pelican doesn't have a traditional
lobby – instead, very sensibly, there
is a bar in the hotel entrance

'Born in the Stars and Stripes' is perfect
for patriotic Republicans (not that
you're likely to meet one here)

Bring your sunglasses: 'Psychedelicate
Girl' is a room for those with a taste for
the wild visuals of the Pop Art sixties

The 'Executive Forties' suite – a long slender room with a corner view of the beach and Ocean Drive

Each room at the Pelican has its own theme and colour scheme: tropical green in the 'Executive Forties' suite

A driftwood lamp is exactly the right kind of kitsch to dress up the 'Executive Fifties' suite

Ruby red and completely over the top, the 'Best Whorehouse' is one of Pelican's most popular rooms

A colourful mosaic typical of the late fifties/early sixties decorates the window sill of the 'Executive Sixties' suite

A twenties poster for a now-defunct brand of cigarettes (in case you wondered where they got the name)

'Up, Up and Away' – a room entirely decorated with bits and pieces of aeroplane

The restaurant's unique style is part roadside diner, part gambling shack, and part industrial warehouse

The 'Executive Fifties' suite: a *Blue Hawaii* kind of interior that faces the beach and Ocean Drive

Life as a guest is certainly an original experience. The fun begins when the sweaty cab that dumped you at the curb (Miami taxis are not air-conditioned) leaves you dragging your suitcases through the Pelican's crowded restaurant, swearing under your breath: 'What do you mean there's no lobby?'

This doesn't seem funny at the time but a few days later when you see another pasty newcomer undergo the same initiation, it suddenly feels like an in-joke. According to the hotel, dragging your bags through the restaurant helps break down 'traditional expectations' – and besides, they really *don't* have much of a lobby. They used the space for the restaurant and bar. It's space well used: the casual atmosphere, courtesy of the 'Honolulu, c. 1954, enlisted men's drinking club' decor, and the generous portions of simple healthy food make it a very easy place to hang out.

In a crazy but charming way, the Pelican takes a gentle swipe at the kitsch underbelly of Miami. Its design is a cheeky take on the crass commercialism of America and Americana. Swedish designer Magnus Ehrland travelled the globe to assemble what must be the single largest collection of modern retro kitsch in the world and used it to create twenty-five themed rooms that play to every fantasy imaginable.

But the seemingly hodgepodge assembly of garage sale items ranging from hula girl lamps to bright orange gothic dining chairs is more sophisticated than it might seem. To hover on the absolute edge of bad taste, without simply being silly and ugly, is not so easy. Like wearing second-hand clothing, you need a lot of confidence and an innate sense of style to carry it off. To stick your creative neck out in this fashion is daring, and Pelican's stylistic bravery has been rewarded with resounding success. Sure, each room is a spoof on the American dream, but they are also unusual, interesting and above all, lots of fun. This, after all, is a hotel, not a home. Why not enjoy a bit of kookiness while you are away? The Pelican is outrageous, but then so is Miami.

---

address Pelican, 826 Ocean Drive, Miami Beach, FL 33139, USA

t +1 (305) 673 3373   **f** +1 (305) 673 3255   **e** pelican@pelicanhotel.com

room rates from US $170

the tides

If the Pelican is South Beach's kooky outsider then the Tides is the smooth newcomer. The ten-storey, all-white Tides is the largest and most imposing structure on Ocean Drive, standing in stately contrast to the other rather squat Art Deco hotels lining Miami's most famous beachside strip. Billed as the first *mature* hotel on South Beach, this whitewashed, ocean-side Art Deco classic (originally opened in 1936) is the jewel in Chris Blackwell's imposing collection of South Beach hotels. It was among the first hotels that he acquired, but interestingly he opted to develop the smaller properties first, saving this – the best – until last.

To launch into what is widely recognized as the second, more refined stage of the continuing rehabilitation of South Beach, Blackwell decided to draw on the services of John Pringle, something of an expert on hotels that pull a good crowd. Between 1951 and 1961 Pringle owned and operated Round Hill, a Jamaican retreat frequented by the likes of the Kennedys, Richard Avedon, Bing Crosby, Alfred Hitchcock, in fact by just about every luminary of the day. 'The secret,' Pringle will confide, 'is to combine low-key guests with anything but low-key service.' The guests are

encouraged to be laid back … the staff are not. It might sound simple enough, but Pringle himself will readily concede that this is not an easy combination to realize.

A distant cousin of Blackwell, Pringle had previously worked as a consultant for his growing hotel empire, but the Tides is the first project in which his involvement, at Blackwell's insistence, was totally hands-on. Not a cushion, curtain or ashtray has escaped Pringle's microscopic attention to detail. Comfort, in his eyes, is only achieved by getting all the details right, small as well as big. And elegant comfort, the kind that appears effortless, was always his aim. This is design by vigilance – a rigorous and disciplined quest to create the kind of place that will attract people accustomed to a certain quality of life. It is not about dazzling them with glitz and glamour but about conjuring up an atmosphere of effortless sophistication.

The Tides is a confident adult alternative for the traveller who appreciates calm as well as frenzy. Calm is the operative word for this place. In contrast to the hectic salsa-driven pace of Ocean Drive, the lobby is as quiet as a soundproof studio. And it is quiet to the eyes as well as the ears: the place is the architectural equivalent of a summer suit,

all cream, beige and off-white, in natural fibres, set against the pale, polished beauty of the original terrazzo floor.

The quiet elegance of the lobby is an appropriate entrée to the Tides' real drawcard, the rooms – or rather the suites, for they are too big to be called rooms. Large, open, all-white and facing the ocean, each is like a tropical loft, a generous whitewashed space with romantic shutters and a clever design that separates off practical facilities such as the closet, mini-bar and changing room, and so allows the main space to remain beautifully unencumbered. Undoubtedly the most remarkable feature is that they all face the beach. When I first heard this I took it to mean some of the rooms, perhaps even most of them. How could each and every one overlook the beach? The answer lies in a drastic remodelling of the interior architecture. The corridor allowing access to the four rooms on each floor was relocated to run along the back of the building (making it the only hotel space with views of the car park to the rear). This no-compromise approach entailed a radical restructuring and the creation of just 45 rooms from 112, a courageous step that would normally be considered bad mathematics in the hotel trade. But for the guest it makes all the difference in the world. In a warm climate, after all, space is directly related to coolness. And a view of the ocean is what everyone wants.

Keeping cool was also a priority in the design of the Serenity Room, the Tides' massage and treatment centre. In the upper reaches of the building, high enough to pick up any trace of a sea breeze, a corner was simply covered over with an awning. El Niño aside, it makes a very attractive proposition.

The guiding aim was to create a discreet and tasteful backdrop to the customers, who Pringle believes 'are more important than any design scheme'. 'A hotel is just like a play', he will tell you: 'if the cast is good, the play is good'.

---

address The Tides, 1220 Ocean Drive Avenue, Miami Beach, FL 33139, USA

t +1 (305) 604 5070   **f** +1 (305) 604 5180   **e** reservations@islandoutpost.com

room rates from US $ 395

four seasons

Armani, Prada, Gucci, Versace, Etro, Dolce & Gabbana … reformed shoppers beware! For you this may be the most dangerous hotel location on earth. Housed in a fifteenth-century Renaissance convent, in the midst of what is known as Milan's 'golden triangle', the Four Seasons is surrounded by all the great names in fashion. This strategic position has proved irresistible to serious shoppers, not to mention the small army of models, agents, editors, buyers and photographers wanting to be part of the splendid design and cosmopolitan atmosphere that is so essentially Milanese.

In reality most of Milan is not like this at all. This is a tough, gritty, industrial city – the engine that drives Italy's economy. As the old saying goes, *Milano lavora e Roma mangia* – the Milanese work, the Romans eat. The mentality of Milan is that of a northern European city. And it is certainly not, with the exception of the old inner city, very pretty. True, it has La Scala and the Duomo, but in general, as a visiting *New York Times* critic so aptly summed it up, 'the city is so grey it makes me want to take it to a carwash'.

Via Gesù no. 8 is a retreat from the grey. Nestled in the city's small but charming medieval core on a quiet street of pale-pink and yellow stately palazzi, Four Seasons envelops its guests in a cocoon of quiet sophistication and restrained beauty. And though this may seem at odds with the city, it is, in reality, a very Milanese phenomenon. If Rome is the 'eternal' city then Milan, the locals will tell you, is the 'internal' city. Everything goes on behind closed doors. Milan's secrets, they say, lie in its courtyards; and the courtyard behind the restrained buttermilk facade of this former palazzo had quite a secret of its own. Acquired in 1987, the property was under extensive reconstruction when first the granite columns, then the vaulted ceilings and eventually the remnants of Flemish-inspired frescoes were uncovered, all belonging to a Renaissance convent. The building had been modernized so often over the centuries that the fifteenth-century convent of Santa Maria del Gesù, to which the street owes its name, was completely buried and forgotten.

As a direct result of this discovery, architect Carlo Meda abandoned his original plans and instead redesigned the hotel to resurrect the architecture of the cloister. The elegant columns that now grace the beautifully restored courtyard give no hint of the sophisticated technology that made all this possible.

Surrounding a magnificent courtyard, the Four Seasons Milan is a haven of peace and quiet in a bustling city

Gilded filigree in the first-floor lift hall is typical of the stylish approach to decoration

Details of the design scheme resemble the early work of Milan's master architect Gio Ponti

Architect Carlo Meda's design revolved entirely around the restoration of the recently rediscovered convent

The colonnaded glory of the original fifteenth-century cloister emerged during excavation of the site

Gilded mirrors and ecclesiastical candlesticks contrast with the simple, modern tones of the lobby

The restaurant, Il Teatro, has become a local favourite. Giorgio Armani is one of many famous regulars

An ornate palazzo ceiling distinguishes Jil Sander's favourite first-floor courtyard room

La Colonna, the less formal café-restaurant, serves Milanese cuisine (with particular focus on desserts)

A corner of the original priory
is now an area designated for
card games

The ground-floor suites retain
the original fifteenth-century
vaulted ceilings

Carefully selected antiques abound,
but the interior never threatens to
become fussy or over-decorated

The library, one of the few public spaces
to retain the original architecture, is
popular for afternoon tea

Unusual detail adorns the hotel's
corridors, such as these remnants
of decorative lace ironwork

Carefully, painstakingly, centuries
of paint were stripped away to reveal
remnants of sixteenth-century frescoes

The seductively shaped oval staircase is
another reminder of Ponti's particular
take on modernist aesthetics

Amenities such as a fully equipped
gymnasium are housed in a large
underground area

By placing utilities like kitchens below
ground, the original courtyard spaces
could be dedicated to guest rooms

Since the original columns could not possibly have carried the load of two floors, a complex, hidden steel skeleton was introduced to provide structural stability. Utilitarian areas such as kitchens, offices, conference rooms and storage were deliberately located below ground so as not to compromise the dimensions of the above-ground cloister. As a result, it was possible to leave intact the magnificent vaulted ceilings of the original fifteenth-century architecture in many of the guest rooms.

But it is not just the good fortune of uncovering a historical jewel that makes this one of the most rewarding hotel experiences in Europe. In a city where the locals are not much partial to visiting hotel lobbies, this refined address on Via Gesù has become an accepted part of Milan's inner scene. La Veranda, the café, is a favourite lunch and aperitif spot among Milan's fashion and banking set, and Il Teatro, presided over by award-winning chef Sergio Mei, is favoured by local luminaries such as Riccardo Muti,

conductor at La Scala, and Giorgio Armani – no doubt because of dishes such as *risotto mantecato con mazzacolle e carciofi alla mentuccia* (imperial prawn risotto with artichokes and peppermint).

If food is a big attraction at Four Seasons, so too is the design. Crisp white walls accented by the odd remnant of a fresco, parquet and terrazzo floors, a beautifully sculptural oval staircase, and Cassina furniture create an atmosphere that recalls the elegant modernism of Gio Ponti, Italy's most celebrated twentieth-century architect. Interestingly, designer Pamela Babey opted *not* to cater to the building's pedigree. As a result there is a total absence of reproduction furniture, heavy fabrics or plush. Instead, modern Italian design is juxtaposed very successfully with the character and charm of the surviving Renaissance architecture. Judging by the sheer volume of shopping bags scattered about the foyer, the only thing it hasn't been able to supply is willpower.

address Four Seasons, Via Gesù 8, 20121 Milan, Italy

t +39 (02) 77088 **f** +39 (02) 7708 5000

room rates from EUR 428.66

soho grand hotel

When it opened in 1996, the SoHo Grand was the first new hotel in SoHo for over a century. This world-famous area of Manhattan, home to the greatest collection of cast-iron architecture in the US, has long resisted any attempt to alter its precious architectural heritage. No wonder then that plans for the SoHo Grand, a structure large enough to house almost four hundred rooms and rising to fifteen storeys (in an area where five or six is the norm), initially met with vigorous local resistance. Yet the inescapable fact is that SoHo really needs a hotel (or two). The area has become vital not just to sections of the art, photographic, design and publishing industries, but also, thanks to the close proximity of New York University, to the academic world too. And anyone who has ever taken a taxi to get to an appointment in SoHo from mid- or uptown hotels will know that arriving on time is about as dependable as getting a cab driver who speaks English.

Unfazed by local objections, proprietor Emanuel Stern took a constructive attitude towards the obstacle of local disapproval. He readily acknowledges that artists are the ones who come in and make an area attractive, while businessmen merely follow in their wake

to capitalize on that. So to ensure that his approach was not seen as exploitative Stern made the smart commitment to root the hotel as much in the local community as possible. In practice this meant employing a SoHo-based designer, working with SoHo-based artists and galleries, and drawing from the SoHo vernacular for the internal as well as the external architecture of the hotel. Stern interviewed fourteen designers before settling on William Sofield, ex-partner in SoHo's trend-setting Aero design studios.

Sofield, whose former work includes creating many of the famously seductive room settings for Ralph Lauren Home, approached this project by blending the area's industrial background with the rich vocabulary of the local architecture. SoHo's famous loft buildings feature Victorian, Italianate, oriental and even Egyptian-inspired embellishment and detailing. Thus the Egyptian columns, oriental lanterns and turn-of-the-century Arts and Crafts ornament that distinguish the SoHo Grand's interior have a secure local precedent.

But it may well have been the constraints placed on Sofield that inspired the true originality and creativity of his scheme. For a host of restrictions was put in the hotel's way.

The ground floor of the SoHo Grand is a raw, muscular space that could double as a set for *Batman*

Vintage Manhattan photography decorates the rooms and is also available for purchase

The pared-down lobby evokes the feeling of America's grand turn-of-the-century railway stations

Arts-and-Crafts-style furniture reflects designer William Sofield's history-conscious approach

The Canal House restaurant, a tall and impressive yet cosy space, specializes in classic American dishes

Despite the scrupulous attention to period detail, there is also a state-of-the-art fitness centre

According to city ordinance, for instance, the ground floor was prohibited from housing any traditional hotel functions because the area is, by legal definition, a flood plain – even though the swamp that prompted this legislation was filled in a century ago. Thus the entrance is quite out of the ordinary, a bit like arriving in a subway station. This brutalist space – an empty cavern dominated by immense brick columns and a staircase of steel girders – serves as an anteroom to the main lobby and reception one floor above. It heightens the impact not just of the lobby, but also of the staircase, embedded with the glass bottle-bottoms traditionally used along the inner edge of sidewalks in the area to illuminate the basements below. It also completely disguises the fact that the ground floor was not allowed to be used as a reception. The design is gutsy, industrial and artistic, an apt metaphor for SoHo itself.

The lobby, an area of appropriately grand proportions, is divided in half by a row of Egyptian-style columns that march across the space in military fashion. One side is strictly business (checking in, checking out, picking up messages), the other (further divided into salon, bar and restaurant) strictly pleasure. With its magnificently high ceilings and monumental proportions (the biggest lamp shades you've ever seen), the restaurant prompted one New York newspaper critic to liken the experience to 'dining in Stalinist Russia'.

Except the food is probably a lot better. In the tradition of many Hip Hotels, the two-star Canal House restaurant is a big drawcard in its own right. Rated by the *New York Times* as 'American food for the knowing diner', its reinvented American classics include Manhattan clam chowder, crab Louis (crab meat with slices of avocado and pink grapefruit), and grilled lamb tenderloin with spoon bread. The atmosphere is cool and calm, a marked departure from the clamour of the SoHo scene – so seductive, in fact, that even the locals who once opposed the hotel so vigorously now regularly drop in for lunch.

address SoHo Grand Hotel, 310 West Broadway, New York, NY 10013, USA
t +1 (212) 965 3000 **f** +1 (212) 965 3200 **e** reservations@sohogrand.com
room rates from US $374

four seasons

In the 1920s, when the US skyscraper boom began in earnest, impossibly tall buildings symbolized the country's mood. The Chrysler Building, Rockefeller Center and the Empire State Building rose as monuments to human ingenuity and energy. These cathedrals of commerce were not only uniquely American – irrefutable proof of America's world leadership in engineering – they were also paragons of promise. Even today, no one could visit New York and fail to be impressed by the skyline. The overwhelming optimism and conviction expressed by the sheer scale and craftsmanship of Manhattan's skyscrapers, particularly the elegant Art Deco originals, remain utterly compelling. In the words of Nathan Silver, author of *Lost New York*, 'an encounter with magnificent architecture irradiates even someone alienated and disaffected'. History, 'the lamp of memory', illuminates these buildings, evoking for each new generation the impressive confidence of a past age.

The 'lamp of memory' is certainly a tool that I.M. Pei makes use of in his architecture, and to dramatic effect. Just as his famous glass pyramid in the courtyard of the Louvre in Paris evokes Napoleon's fascination with ancient Egypt, I.M. Pei's design for the Four Seasons Hotel evokes heroic New York – the days when the glamour, confidence and sheer craftsmanship of the American skyscraper symbolized America's world dominance in engineering and were a testament to the overwhelming success of capitalism.

I.M. Pei seems to understand very well the irresistibility of buildings imbued with history. For that is the power of the Four Seasons. Walk into the lobby, with its massive bronze urns, intricate marble floor and spectacular onyx ceiling soaring ten metres above the entrance hall, and you are instantly transported back to the glamour and prosperity of the twenties. With this new skyscraper – which at fifty-two floors is the tallest hotel in New York – he has truly captured the original magic of Manhattan. And in reinventing the classic American skyscraper he has observed the tradition of quality as well as scale. This is a building that makes no attempt to hide its intention to impress, but it does so through the timeless qualities of monumental scale and superb craftsmanship. The confidence communicated by its architecture is certainly infectious. No wonder the Four Seasons Hotel is so consistently popular, and with locals as well as out-of-towners.

'Noo Yawkers' are infamous as the most critical audience in the world, so it is a real testament to this hotel that they flock to meet in its bar for drinks (the Four Seasons' 'French martini' and 'citrus martini' lead the field), to sample the cuisine in the Fifty Seven Fifty Seven Restaurant (awarded a three-star rating from the *New York Times*, unprecedented for a hotel dining room) and to meet friends for a quick pre-theatre supper in the Lobby Restaurant. In the morning they will even stand in line for a breakfast table. Taste the lemon and ricotta hotcakes and you'll understand why. In short, the Four Seasons has become something of a hangout, and not just for chief executives and producer types slavishly accustomed to the immaculate level of service and impressive standard of food, but also for locals who work in the neighbourhood and for the film stars who like to linger in the lobby waiting to protest at being recognized.

Then there are the guest rooms straight out of those old black-and-white movies set in swanky Manhattan, where men are always in black tie, and impossibly elegant women in long glittering dresses drape themselves around handsome interiors. Double the size of the average New York hotel room, they have sweeping views of the sparkling city below, showing New York exactly the way you always imagined it to be: big, glamorous and impressive. Some even have their own terrace, which, particularly on the upper floors, can be quite something. Yet large and luxurious as they are, they are not overdone. Care was taken to emulate the stylistic atmosphere of American Art Deco without merely reconstructing the past. A very contemporary clarity and simplicity, in sophisticated shades of sand and bronze, is what you get at the Four Seasons New York.

So is the Four Seasons Hotel more expensive because of all this glamour, luxury and space? Who cares? As one prominent New York travel agent observed, 'The Four Seasons is like a Broadway hit. Everyone wants to go. No matter what the price.'

address Four Seasons, 57 East 57th Street, New York, NY 10022, USA

t +1 (212) 758 5700 **f** +1 (212) 758 5711

room rates from US$435

the mercer

A decade ago André Balazs, hotel and nightclub impresario and proprietor of LA's Chateau Marmont, acquired an imposing red-brick building on the corner of Spring and Mercer Streets in the heart of trendy SoHo and announced plans to open a hotel. Much delayed and postponed, its opening became the most eagerly anticipated event in Manhattan. The question everyone was asking was 'was it worth the wait?' The answer is an unequivocal yes. Why? Because it is entirely unlike any other hotel in New York, if not the world.

By preserving the windows, the ceiling height and the proportions of the warehouse space, the Mercer is the first hotel to offer a taste of 'loft living', an urban signature that is completely original to New York. The conventional notion of a hotel room has been abandoned. Instead every room feels like a loft, with the seductive qualities of unencumbered space and abundant natural light – exactly what attracted the community of artists who first gave this area its distinctive character.

The only problem with a loft space is how to furnish it. A loft demands a design approach that enhances rather than fills the space. That is why Balazs chose to work with Parisian designer Christian Liaigre. His combination of handsome, pared-down furniture in African Wenge wood, neutrally toned textiles, simple lamps, dark wooden floors, pure white walls, crisp white linen, and a hint of lilac leather on elegant banquettes is exactly what was needed – a subtle, clean and classic approach that steers clear of furniture fashion and design clichés.

The design commitment to the loft experience is absolute, and continues with the bathrooms. The Mercer has the best bathrooms in North America. Period. This is not just because they're all white marble and white mosaic tile or because they're incredibly spacious, with a centrally placed bath and a stylish stainless-steel trolley for towels and cosmetics. It is because they are so cleverly integrated into the overall space. What, after all, is the point of going to great lengths (not to mention expense) to preserve the integrity of a warehouse loft space if the bathroom is then relegated to a pokey little cubicle? At the Mercer the bathrooms are open to, and part of, the overall interior. Although there are folding doors to provide privacy and partition when so required, why use them when taking a bath in full view of the surrounding space and the buildings across the street is such a seductive highlight – so urban, so decadent, so SoHo?

Almost like a Pop Art installation, the end of each corridor is defined by a different colour

In the Mercer's startlingly white bathrooms, the simplest touch of colour stands out

The restrained yet dramatic use of colour in the corridors mimics that in the rooms

A massive square bath illuminated by an overhead light well is typical of the top-floor bathrooms

Colour is used sparingly, like jewelry – just enough for effect. Even the hues are reminiscent of pale gemstones

Large, white, spacious and refined, the Mercer has what many critics agree are the best bathrooms in the US

A corner room with Liaigre-designed chairs and the Mercer's trademark oval conversation table

African Wenge wood, Carrara marble surfaces and white walls are Christian Liaigre's signature ingredients

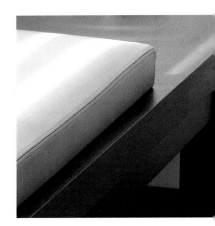

Slim banquettes upholstered in lilac leather are an elegant touch in the all-white interiors

Wherever possible, the cast-iron pillars of the nineteenth-century warehouse building were left in position

Instead of the usual desk that nobody uses, Liaigre provided each and every room with a generous oval table

Every detail, even the wall-mounted bedside lamp, was custom-made for the Mercer

Pale green and lilac are perfect colours to complement the clean white of this uncompromisingly urban environment

The beds are immaculate, with neutral-shaded linen covers and Frette sheets. Who wants to rough it in a loft?

Dark African Wenge wood contrasts with modern bone china and orange raffia place mats

All the rooms, even the smallest, have that distinctly urban feeling of a loft space

Daylight is what makes SoHo so special – it is the only area of Manhattan without (sun-blocking) skyscrapers

The stainless-steel trolley equipped with towels and cosmetics is standard to all Mercer bathrooms

SoHo (*South of Hou*ston Street) is unique in Manhattan because it's the only area without skyscrapers. The tallest buildings are a modest six storeys, allowing daylight to filter in and so avoiding the dark canyons that dominate the rest of New York City. Once upon a time these light-filled warehouses, with their acres of space, were inhabited almost exclusively by industry. Then, after a period of neglect and abandonment, they were discovered by artists, who moved in and transformed the buildings and the area too. Now it's a different story. The last couple of decades have seen the price of a SoHo loft pull just about even with the price of an Upper East Side apartment. Struggling artists can definitely no longer afford to live here. Yet though much vilified (particularly by the art community) this gentrification of SoHo has helped create the environment that now sustains some of Manhattan's best boutiques, restaurants and bars.

Despite the competition, Balazs has boldly thrown his hat into the ring. The Mercer Kitchen, a restaurant located in the basement of the building, creates the feel of eating in the kitchen, 'always the best setting for conversation among the best of friends' according to Balazs. Illuminated by glass bottle-bottoms embedded in the sidewalk overhead (very characteristic of the area), the ambience combined with the cuisine of chef Jean-Georges Vongerichten has made The Mercer Kitchen one of the most consistently popular and fashionable restaurants in SoHo.

The matt-black crowd of ad agency staff, art directors, photographers and fashion people may have shunted out the artists, but SoHo still has an attitude and an atmosphere you won't find with the 'big coat, small poodle' crowd on the Upper East Side. For Nathan Silver, author of *Lost New York*, 'if anything should stand forever as a radiant image of the essential New York, it ought to be these [SoHo's] commercial buildings.' Continually evolving in response to contemporary needs, they are 'the best and purest that New York has to offer.'

---

address The Mercer, 147 Mercer Street, New York, NY 10012, USA

t +1 (212) 966 6060 **f** +1 (212) 965 3838

room rates from US$395

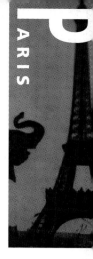

hôtel costes

Jean Louis Costes is no shrinking violet. In the early eighties he set all of Paris talking by opening a new café – a café that broke all the rules. It had no chandeliers, no mirrors, no fancy Belle Epoque embellishment and no address worth mentioning. Situated on the corner of the distinctly unfashionable rue St-Denis, near Les Halles (an area better known for its ladies of the night), and designed by a then complete unknown (a former art director at Christian Dior named Philippe Starck), Café Costes nevertheless became a huge hit. It was *the* place in Paris. The men's toilet became just about the most photographed space in the history of interior design, Italian furniture manufacturer Driade sold almost a million of the café's trademark 'Costes chairs', and Philippe Starck became something of a national hero.

Almost twenty years later Jean Louis Costes has done it again. Everyone is talking about Hôtel Costes and its *wunderkind* designer Jacques Garcia. Situated on the ultra chichi rue St-Honoré, this is the place where all of Paris is having lunch. Ditto dinner. Even other hotels send their guests here. It is *the* place to go for pre-dinner *apéritifs* or after-dinner *digestifs*. It is where public relations firms

arrange press interviews for their celebrity clients. It's a scene … and a circus. But what a circus! Hôtel Costes rekindles the exaggerated styles and atmosphere of France's Second Empire. History meets fantasy in eccentrically decorated spaces that surround a courtyard straight out of an aristocrat's palazzo. A small, dark, intimate dining room created in a style best described as 'oriental opium den' is next to the 'Herbarium', a perfect lunchtime retreat decorated wall to wall with mounted and framed pharmacological leaves. Yet another dining room is in the exaggerated neoclassical style of the late nineteenth century. For winter days there's a cosy space isolated by thick curtains arranged around a monumental fantasy of a fireplace, as well as the opportunity to dine in the glass-enclosed corridors surrounding the courtyard like a circular greenhouse.

This powerful mix of texture, colour, pattern and historic period is the speciality and the passion of interior designer Jacques Garcia. Neoclassicism, orientalism, Empire Revival: these are his decorative hallmarks – preferably mixed. His love of excess is in evidence throughout the hotel: in the corridors, the guest suites, the bathrooms.

A magnificent Belle Epoque fireplace warms one of the winter dining rooms of Hôtel Costes

Bathroom floors in richly coloured, ornate tiles satisfy designer Jacques Garcia's penchant for orientalism

In the lobby you feel as if you are waiting for a train in an Agatha Christie novel

No detail has been overlooked: the classical statues were cast in modern plastic and painted to appear old

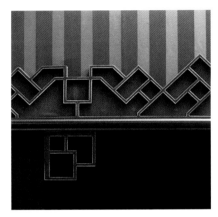

Garcia is a master at mixing texture, pattern and colour, particularly if they have historic precedents

The light-filled corridor that runs along the courtyard is used for winter lunches

Pattern on pattern on pattern – Garcia's approach creates a luxurious atmosphere

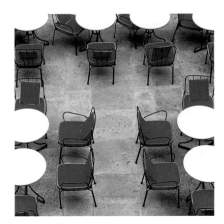

Fifties chairs straight out of *La Dolce Vita* create a certain Latin ambience on the terrace of the hotel's courtyard

The reception desk, where guests can sit down to check in, is in the ornate style of the Belle Epoque

The bathrooms are the only reminder that this is the twentieth century – but then only in terms of plumbing, not style

The stools that furnish the Chinese-opium-den-inspired bar are typical of Jacques Garcia's attention to detail

The courtyard is like that of an old Tuscan palazzo belonging to an eccentric Italian count

Garcia designed the furniture himself. These turn-of-the-century salon chairs feature in different fabrics and colours

A popular spot for afternoon tea, the Herbarium is decorated with framed pharmacological specimens

Designer Jacques Garcia is opposed to the trend towards simplicity; he prefers the more seductive quality of complexity

Hidden in the catacombs, the gym has every machine and gadget any gym junkie could dream of

Mirrors, flower paintings and a chinoiserie trellis frame the door leading into the opium-den bar

A neoclassically inspired room decorated with Egyptian Revivalist touches is one of six ground-floor restaurant spaces

Even the amazing subterranean pool, buried in the catacombs, does not escape his talent for staging drama and fantasy. 'Why,' jokes Garcia, 'do things simply, when you can make them more complicated?'

All the decorative Belle Epoque details, so scrupulously omitted from Café Costes, are reintroduced with abandon in Hôtel Costes. No trace of Monsieur Starck here. Jean Louis Costes clearly demands originality, even if that means reinventing the past. If everyone else is going modern, he seems to be saying, I'll go antique. Thus the unexpected choice of Jacques Garcia as designer. Previously known only to the most exclusive circles of super-rich French society, Garcia is the man who uses his encyclopaedic knowledge of the decorative arts to create period environments more fantastic than they perhaps ever were. As journalist Philippe Seulliet explained in a recent profile, 'he creates rooms which seem to bear the traces of generations but are, in fact, the product of his inspired and gently irreverent imagination.'

Extensively published in the more rarefied interiors magazines, his best-known projects such as Château Champ de Bataille in Normandy have, in the main, been for himself. Hôtel Costes was an opportunity to give his distinct signature a more commercial and populist expression. To create its sensual, multilayered, tapestry-like environment, Garcia commissioned all the lamps, furniture, fabrics, wallpaper and floor coverings to be custom-made. With the exception of some fabrics and wallpapers produced by a small, highly specialized English firm, there is nothing in Hôtel Costes that can be purchased in a shop. That is one reason why the result is so striking. Garcia has taken a style that had been generally regarded as pure personal indulgence, even folly, and translated it to the pragmatic and unforgiving world of commercial design. The result is a great success, betraying no sign of compromise or unsuitability.

So, forget the Bauhaus dictum 'less is more'. Start thinking 'too much is never enough'.

address Hôtel Costes, 239 rue Saint-Honoré, 75001 Paris, France

t +33 (1) 4244 5000 **f** +33 (1) 4244 5001

room rates from 2,000 FF

l'hôtel

For over four decades, L'Hôtel has been a style institution – a hotel as legendary as its Left Bank location. It could be said that this place on the Rue des Beaux-Arts was one of the world's first Hip Hotels. It has always been a favourite of more adventurous travellers in search of the daring and the different. Ever since American decorator Robin Westbrook transformed the old hotel in the 1960s into a veritable chocolate box of decorative themes – ranging from 'all-over leopard skin' to '1930s mirrored deco' – it has stood out as reassuringly quirky and fancifully independent. In a period in which chains such as Hilton were luring guests with blatant uniformity (same room, anywhere in the world), L'Hôtel was investing in total individuality. It's difficult now to grasp just how far ahead of its time such an approach was back in the 1960s.

But time moves on, and even the most successful design schemes eventually need updating. Even so, there was a collective shudder when the new owner, Guy-Louis Duboucheron, announced his intention of giving the historic hotel a complete makeover. After all, there was more at stake here than the wallpaper. As the plaque outside affirms, this was the place where Oscar Wilde died – just

weeks after penning his famously prescient line 'I am dying beyond my means.' Broke, sick, his reputation in tatters, his legendary wit was still razor-sharp.

Historically speaking, L'Hôtel is a heavyweight in the world of Hip Hotels, and any plan to tart it up was never going to get a smooth reception. That said, it was high time for some improvements – the old girl really did need it. By the late 1990s, many of the rooms were borderline shabby and, although there was room service, the hotel had long since given up operating a bar or a restaurant. It was great for people looking to strike out on their own or for aesthetes who relish the unconventional, but it was rather short on comforts for the rest of us. L'Hôtel had withered to little more than a great staircase and some wild rooms in a splendid location.

Now, following a top-to-bottom makeover by Jacques Garcia (renowned designer of Hôtel Costes) L'Hôtel can offer a whole array of top-class facilities: a restaurant and a bar on the neo-classically inspired ground floor, plus a swimming pool and spa in the once-creepy catacombs below the building. Such additions have without doubt made this Left Bank venue an infinitely more comfortable place to stay.

But more impressive still is the sense of continuity between the old design scheme and the new. If you didn't know the old L'Hôtel, you really wouldn't know much had changed. New spaces such as the restaurant are so convincingly authentic in ambience and detail that they defy anyone to remember how they might once have been. To the credit of Messieurs Duboucheron and Garcia, some of the most important rooms have been restored rather than revamped. Number 16, Oscar Wilde's room, is still reassuringly Victorian and English in its aesthetic; the Orientalist atmosphere of room 40 so beloved of writer Pierre Loti has been preserved; and the sexy mirrored detailing of red, white and blue room number 36, favourite of singer Mistinguett, is still intact.

Architecturally speaking, the highlight of the hotel remains its magnificent stairwell, a round neoclassical internal tower decorated with plaster medallions which rises from a star-patterned inlaid stone floor towards a dome that is open to the sky. Installed by Westbrook in the 1960s, there is absolutely nothing else like it in Paris – yet it is the kind of *folie* that is perfectly at home in an address on the Rue des Beaux-Arts.

This, after all, is the beating heart of the Left Bank, the the Paris of Ernest Hemingway, Pablo Picasso, Gertrude Stein, Man Ray, F. Scott Fitzgerald and so many other legendary artists and writers. Just walking the streets is a form of sophisticated cultural voyeurism. It is still possible here to imagine yourself in the Beatnik Paris of the fifties and sixties. Everywhere there are beautiful little shops specializing in rare books and artifacts; small galleries that hold big openings which inevitably spill out onto the stone-cobbled streets; and the odd design boutique with a minimalist display showing off the latest in fashion for the home. For window shopping, for sitting in cafés and watching life go by, for squeezing the most out of what the Left Bank has to offer there's no better location in Paris.

address L'Hôtel, 13 rue des Beaux-Arts, 75006 Paris, France

t +33 (1) 44 41 99 00 **f** +33 (1) 43 25 64 81 **e** reservation@l-hotel.com

room rates from 1,550 FF

hôtel lancaster

'Grown-up glamour' is how Grace Leo-Andrieu likes to describe her hotel. It's hard to disagree. Hotel Lancaster may well be the most glamorous hotel in Paris. Not because it dazzles you with glitz – it's too discreet for that. This is not the Ritz. It doesn't employ a small army of uniformed staff and there is no 'scene' in the lobby. But that is exactly the point. The Lancaster, as Leo-Andrieu sees it, is for people who have nothing left to prove. If you're past impressing people with where you are staying, then you're ready for the more subtle pleasures of a hotel that US *Town & Country* magazine recently described as 'the most sophisticated, refined hotel experience in Paris'.

The understated luxury and timeless quality of the Lancaster have long been attracting international celebrities, including Cary Grant, Grace Kelly and Clark Gable. Marlene Dietrich virtually made this her Paris home: one of the suites is named after her and decorated entirely in her favourite colour, lilac. Yet despite its high-profile clientele, the Lancaster has always been very low profile, and Leo-Andrieu intends to keep it that way. Quite simply, the hotel is for hotel guests only. The dining room, for example – idyllically situated overlooking a splendid courtyard garden – is not open to the public. Period. Hotel Lancaster consequently feels more like a club than a hotel. Here, as a guest, you are free to entertain, drink or dine without the rest of the world watching and without having to compete with them for a table booking.

Private and beautifully decorated, the Lancaster has a style all its own. The first proprietor to convert this grand Haussmann-era apartment building (four floors, four apartments) into a hotel was Emile Wolf, a Swiss gentleman with a rather fine eye who was helped in his treasure hunt for the hotel by the fact that his housekeeper's father was an antique dealer. Endless visits to Paris auctions, antique stalls and flea markets brought superb Baccarat crystal, tapestries, Louis XV and XVI chairs and countless other fine pieces to the hotel. M. Wolf, it seems, was also something of a clock aficionado and today every other room features a piece from his remarkable collection. The same is true of the work of the Russian court portraitist Boris Pastoukhoff, a White Russian who was forced into exile by the revolution and ended up in Paris. During the twenties and early thirties Pastoukhoff would often make the Lancaster his home, using his talent to pay his way.

Some of the bathrooms of Hotel Lancaster were restored to recreate the glamorous twenties originals

The bar: vintage champagne, avant-garde photography books, and a Thai silk lamp

The porte-cochère of this Haussmann-era apartment building is now an elegantly minimal entrance

The original proprietor, Monsieur Emile Wolf, had a passion for collecting clocks

The Dietrich Suite is entirely decorated in shades of Marlene's favourite colour, lilac

The courtyard garden was completely redesigned in a more modern, more exotic, eastern style

As a result the hotel ended up owning nearly eighty oil paintings by an artist whose work is also to be found in the permanent collections of top museums around the world, including the Brooklyn Museum of Fine Arts and the Museo Reina Sofia in Madrid.

Emile Wolf certainly left behind an impressive legacy, but by the time Grace Leo-Andrieu purchased the property in 1996 the hotel was in dire need of modernization. A panel of respected experts was consulted as to how best to restore the antiques, and the priceless pieces were carefully repaired. Old, tired upholstery was replaced by plain silks in oriental tones of mauve, lilac, pink and ochre. Contemporary pieces by designers such as Christian Liaigre were introduced, as were collections of chinoiserie coffee tables, Japanese lacquered nests of tables, cachepots of orchids, celadon bowls and specially commissioned Chinese ink portraits in the dining room. The result is the most seductive kind of environment of all – a mix of the modern, the antique and the oriental. It's an exotic blend – just like its owner. Grace Leo-Andrieu made her name in the world of hotels with highly individual, cosmopolitan places like the Guanahani in St Barts, the Clarence in Dublin and the Paris Left Bank Hotel Montalembert. Born in Hong Kong (to hotelier parents), educated in the United States, and married to a Frenchman, Leo-Andrieu translated her mixed cultural experiences into one of the most exciting hotels to open in Paris in the nineties. But what she created is not only different, it is also very professional, and nothing less than traditional in its standards of service.

Grace Leo-Andrieu remembers when, fresh out of Cornell Hotel School, she was working at the Warwick Hotel just next door. Every time she walked past the sleepy Lancaster with its doorman lazily smoking out front she would imagine all the things she would do 'if I could get my hands on that place'. A decade later she did.

---

address Hôtel Lancaster, 7 rue de Berri, 75008 Paris, France

t +33 (1) 40 76 40 76   **f** +33 (1) 40 76 40 00   **e** reservations@hotel-lancaster.fr

room rates from EUR 400

hôtel montalembert

In a city that boasts as many hotels as Paris, it is difficult to believe that until recently the choice was rather limited. You could live it up in grand Right Bank style (if you could afford it) or settle for the cosy, quaint charms of the Left Bank – exposed beams, low ceilings and minuscule bathrooms (if at all). Aristocrats and powerbrokers stayed grand; tourists stayed quaint. It worked rather well. But then a new breed of traveller started to appear: the frequent flyer, a thoroughly modern professional with thoroughly modern needs. The Montalembert was the first hotel to cater specifically to this new type – without sacrificing the personality of Paris.

Situated on rue de Montalembert – named after the comte de Montalembert, the great nineteenth-century writer and orator – this historic limestone landmark was built in 1926. Located just off the boulevard St-Germain, a quick stroll from the famous Café Deux Magots and Café Flore, the Montalembert has been a favourite with artists and writers since its inception. Yet by the time the property was acquired in 1990 by Grace Leo-Andrieu and her husband Stephane, the hotel was so much on the decline that it looked more like a fusty, nondescript government building. After a nine-month, eight-million dollar restoration, Hotel Montalembert reopened under the direction of Leo-Andrieu's pace-setting hotel company, with, as Christian Liaigre puts it, 'the soul it never had'. It also opened just in time, noted *Gourmet* magazine, 'to take up the slack left by the demise of the much-loved Hotel Pont Royal', whose bar had been a literary Mecca, frequented by the area's publishers and authors.

The goal of the Montalembert renovation was simple: to integrate a distinct, contemporary style with the elegant original architecture of the building. The hotel's collection of antique pieces was restored; Liaigre's furniture designs were installed throughout the fifty-one rooms and five suites; and sculptor Eric Schmitt was commissioned to produce the 'neo-barbaric' bronze wall lights. But the greatest success of the Montalembert's reinvention has to be the ground-floor space. A café, restaurant, cosy library and bar were eked out of an area not much bigger than a small apartment. This is no mere breakfast nook for hotel guests, but a fully functional series of independent spaces. Defined not by partitions, which would have turned the area into a rabbit warren, but by different levels of light intensity, these spaces have become an authentic Left Bank hangout.

The Montalembert's restaurant has become a popular lunch-time haunt for the neighbourhood's *antiquaires* and *littérateurs*. The food is like the design – a mix of the modern and the classic. New cuisine includes salmon with fresh herbs and sautéed chicken in sherry vinegar with braised courgettes, while French classics include *lapin à la moutarde à l'ancien*. In the winter the fireside book-lined space adjoining the restaurant is a perfect, and popular, spot for afternoon tea, served from an impressive array of tisanes by the city's best tea purveyors, Mariage Frères. And in summer the bamboo of the small garden adjoining the library beckons for early evening aperitifs.

Designer Christian Liaigre is no longer so enamoured with the eye-catching marine and taupe rug depicting the count's handwriting that paves the way into the hotel, but the Montalembert has certainly not lost any of the appeal that made it *le must de Paris* in the early nineties. In fact this hotel is a convincing argument for the wisdom of Grace Leo-Andrieu's signature approach of adhering to a simple palette of unpretentious luxury. From the oak floors to the Italian marble in the bathrooms, from the monogrammed Frette linen to the flowers by Christian Tortu (the most stylish florist in Paris), every detail reflects her commitment to a consistent but contemporary sense of quality. Guests have a choice between traditional with a hint of modern (refurbished Louis Philippe antiques with the odd modern lamp and Liaigre chair) or completely modern rooms furnished in the solid sycamore timber designs that typify Liaigre's measured minimalism.

Steeped in Left Bank culture, the Montalembert feels like the Paris from a book. And that is because it is: in Nancy Mitford's *The Pursuit of Love* the Montalembert is the romantic 'secret' tucked off the boulevard St-Germain; and in Peter Mayle's novel *Chasing Cézanne* it is the epitome of chic, the logical place for the hero, a photographer for glossy magazines, to hide out.

address Hôtel Montalembert, 3 rue de Montalembert, 75007 Paris, France
t +33 (1) 45 49 68 68   **f** +33 (1) 45 49 69 49   **e** welcome@hotel-montalembert.fr
room rates from EUR 320

hotel locarno

Small, intimate, stylish and highly individual, Hotel Locarno has consistently been voted the best three-star hotel in Rome … and by Italian newspapers and magazines, no less. It is also a firm favourite with the film industry. In fact, with its Belle Epoque birdcage lift, crumbling terrazzo floor and genuine Art Nouveau bentwood furniture, it could be a film set. This is the kind of place where dark-haired women clad in clinging black and Manolo Blahnik mules arrive on the back of motorbikes and disappear into the lift, never to be seen again. With the outward appearance of a setting in an Agatha Christie novel, Hotel Locarno is a genuine enigma: though almost always full, you hardly ever see anyone, and when you do they almost inevitably slink away quietly at the slightest hint of someone else's arrival. It's one of the few places I've stayed where almost nobody turns up for breakfast. This is no place for early risers, nor for business meetings or power breakfasts.

The interior of the hotel reflects the fact that the owners, a mother-daughter team, have travelled extensively throughout Europe (and continue to do so) in search of antiques to furnish it. Over the years they have assembled quite a collection of Art Nouveau, Belle Epoque and Art Deco pieces, the periods they are most passionate about. In fact, the Locarno is really a never-ending design project for Maria Teresa Celli and her daughter Caterina Valente. The dining room, with its winter fireplace, features an impressive array of original Thonet bentwood furniture, as does the bar and the smaller winter breakfast room overlooking the courtyard garden. Even the windows facing the street were specially commissioned from an architect in the Nouveau style. They are so convincing that one would swear they have been there since the turn of the century. The hotel also has a sixth-floor roof garden with a commanding view over the River Tiber and the domes of the church tops in the Piazza del Popolo. During the summer months, which in Rome begin as early as March, breakfast is served on the roof terrace. It would be a perfect place to start the day, if only some of the guests would wake up in time.

In a city with more than its fair share of tourism this is one of the few hotels that doesn't feel, look or act like a tourist trap. Considerable effort has clearly been put into this place, and the resulting ambience attracts a crowd that appreciates its individualism.

The bar and restaurant of Hotel Locarno feature an extraordinary collection of turn-of-the-century bentwood furniture

Old iron bedheads and antique tables typify the individual design approach – no two guest rooms are alike

A stone bird bath found by proprietor Maria Teresa Celli is now the basin in the restaurant bathroom

With a view of the street and courtyard, the Art Nouveau bar is popular for early morning espresso or late night grappa

The film noir atmosphere of the Locarno has made it a hang-out for artists, actors and photographers

The roof terrace with views over the church spires of Piazza del Popolo is the summer location for breakfast

It is also blessed with a great location, an added plus in a city where you should – indeed must – walk. How else could you stumble across one of those great little restaurants hidden in an alleyway and frequented only by locals? On foot (or perhaps on a Vespa) is the only way.

Hotel Locarno is just off Piazza del Popolo, the largest square in Rome, and located at the beginning of Via del Corso, so shopping is within easy striking distance. But first you may want to stop for a cappuccino, or a light lunch at Rosati, an elegant tea room and café overlooking the entire square. Piazza del Popolo is listed in almost every book about Rome as a great place to sit on the terrace of a café and do some serious people-watching. It's the perfect spot to bask in the sun, watch the world go by and enjoy the luxury of being in the company of Romans as well as tourists.

Then there's the shopping. Walk and window shop along Via del Corso until you reach the Spanish Steps, whereupon you might want to head down Via Condotti for the bigger name label shops, such as Gucci, Prada and of course Rome's own, Valentino. Now that you are among the tourists you might as well give in and stop at Caffè Greco, a Rome institution for afternoon tea since the mid-eighteenth century, and still well worth a visit.

The message is clear: for people who make their own fun, who don't rely on hotels to pamper them and arrange everything, Hotel Locarno is the place. Popular with writers, photographers, film makers and musicians, it feels more like a film noir apartment building than a conventional hotel.

As *Vogue* points out, 'Rome's hotel trade has always been a lucrative one – with a steady captive market of cultural and religious pilgrims, most of the city's hoteliers have found it unnecessary to lavish money, care or imagination on their establishments. There are scores of seedy hotels occupying picturesque old convents, palaces and villas, but there are only a few small hotels of genuine charm and good quality.' Hotel Locarno is definitely one.

---

address Hotel Locarno, Via della Penna 22, 00186 Rome, Italy

t +39 (06) 361 08 41   **f** +39 (06) 321 52 49   **e** info@hotellocarno.com

room rates from L240,000

the phoenix

Squeezed in among the dirty brown buildings, massage parlours and X-rated movie houses of San Francisco's seedy (*Buzz* magazine prefers the word 'spicy') Tenderloin area, the Phoenix is definitely in the shabby end of town. First-time visitors, drawn by the hotel's rock and roll reputation, often arrive convinced the taxi-driver has made a mistake. But face it, if you want a hotel with some attitude, you're not going to find it in the chichi neighbourhoods.

The Phoenix is a hot favourite with the music world, and with all its press and media attention, as well as its dubious location, has earned itself quite a name as the bad boy of downtown 'Frisco hotels (a reputation that has only helped make it even more popular). There are plenty of stories about all the goings on at the Phoenix, and some are true – such as the time a reggae band threw all the plants in the pool – though most probably have less to do with truth than with selling newspapers. One fact, however, is undisputed. Rock stars like staying here. Just ask Sonic Youth, the Red Hot Chili Peppers, Radiohead, the Beastie Boys, Erasure, David Bowie, the Hoodoo Gurus, REM, Ziggy Marley, Sinead O'Connor, Debbie Harry or Tracy Chapman, to name but a few. And it's not hard to understand why. The area

is not too 'delicate' and the hotel has a big car park. Guests can make a lot of noise *and* their roadies won't have to worry about where to park the rig.

But the Phoenix is not just a hotel for bands who can't get in anywhere else. The roster of famous non-rock-star guests is almost embarrassingly respectable, including such unexpected names as John Kennedy Jr. So what's the big attraction? Very simply, the Phoenix is cool. In appearance, it's your classic all-American motel, just like the ones in the movies (*Thelma and Louise* or *Pulp Fiction* come to mind). Only this motel happens to be smack bang in the middle of the city. Rescued in the late eighties by hotel entrepreneur Chip Conley (who also created Hotel Rex) from its previous status as an hourly stopover for hookers and from the possible fate of the wrecking ball, it has every appearance of being a textbook American motor lodge. But it's not. Hiding behind a salmon-pink and turquoise fifties facade pretending to be a plain all-American motel is a carefully considered, art-filled environment. Like Andy Warhol's soup cans or Roy Lichtenstein's cartoon paintings, it's a familiar American icon remade to convey a new message.

With the addition of an enormous mural by New York artist Francis Forlenza, which covers an entire wall of an adjoining building, as well as some 250 other pieces of contemporary art that were introduced throughout the hotel, something completely new was created from something so familiar. Do the guests get it? Anthony Kiedis, lead singer of the Red Hot Chili Peppers, certainly appears to. He describes the Phoenix as 'the most sexually, intellectually and culturally stimulating hotel in San Francisco'.

Yet during the day the Phoenix is dead. In fact you would never know that the hotel was full. But that's just because everyone is still asleep. Only at night does the Phoenix, true to its name, start to come back to life. And once it does, the hotel bar and restaurant, Backflip, is the place to be. Designed in the style of a late-fifties Las Vegas cocktail bar, Backflip is like a permanent poolside party. With exotic private cabanas, a mirror-tiled fireplace, blue plastic banquettes, plastic fifties furniture and a bank of spot-lit fountains, Backflip permanently has the energy levels and high-octane atmosphere of a record launch. It's impossibly busy, impossibly trendy and impossibly difficult to get in. As a hotel guest, however, you not only have the benefit of assured entry but also the distinct convenience of only having to stagger across the courtyard to get to your room at the end of the night.

And what about the rooms? There are forty-four of them, each decorated in 'tropical bungalow style'. And, appropriately, they all look out over the 35-foot elliptical painted pool entitled 'My Fifteen Minutes – Tumbling Waves'. The rooms combine a collection of paintings by up-and-coming artists with tropicana kitsch – imported bamboo furniture, eye-height bird-of-paradise plants, and a palette of bright island colours that create a warm, inviting atmosphere that guests seem to grow fond of rather quickly. Even so, as they say, 'if you can remember your room, you probably didn't stay at the Phoenix'.

address The Phoenix, 601 Eddy Street, San Francisco, California 94109, USA

t +1 (415) 776 1380   **f** +1 (415) 885 3109   **e** info@phoenixhotel.com

room rates from US $109

hotel rex

Hotel Rex has the ambience of a literary haunt. Although newly opened, this hotel feels like the setting of a thirties American film. It's the kind of place Bogey or Robert Mitchum would have felt comfortable, with a moody, mysterious feel just right for a rugged detective in a raincoat. It's a reminder of a type of hotel that hasn't been seen since John Huston's *The Maltese Falcon*.

The Rex has real atmosphere. It feels like a hotel for writers, and that is exactly what was intended. Acquired in September 1996 by the Joie de Vivre group, a specialist San Francisco-based small hotel group which also owns and operates the Phoenix and the Commodore Hotel, the former Orchard Hotel was completely redesigned with the aim of turning it into a West Coast recreation of the 1920s Algonquin, the legendary haunt of Dorothy Parker and New York's fast-moving, high-living literary set.

References to literature dominate the interior design. There is a small lobby bar, but no separate restaurant. Instead there is a library complete with leather-bound first editions and yards of solid mahogany cabinets, shelving and panelling. Surrounded by books, this is where guests are served breakfast in the morning, literary lunches are held during the day and people gather for drinks in the evening. The cosy but sophisticated bookish atmosphere of this ground-floor meeting place is enhanced by an impressive collection of thirties Californian art, handpainted lamp shades and big, comfortable, monogrammed club chairs.

The literary theme continues in the corridors with quotes from Dashiell Hammett and John Steinbeck decorating the walls, while the lift doors feature a collage of pages from the social registrars of the interwar period. In a radical departure from the pretty-pretty bedrooms of most small hotels, the rooms at the Rex are bold, simple and very masculine. A dark maroon carpet with royal blue and yellow stripes is combined with dark polished timber pieces and bedspreads in checks of green and white. And for the larger rooms, the furniture and ambience are once again bookish.

Prime location is a key aspect of the Rex's appeal. It is situated on Sutter Street, known for its galleries and antique shops, while Union Square, Chinatown and all of San Francisco's most glamorous shops and restaurants are only a short stroll from the front door. The central business district is also within easy walking distance, and the hotel offers a fully serviced dining room for special functions and conferences.

Hotel Rex has quickly made a name on the SF arts scene. It has acted as host hotel for the San Francisco International Film Festival and has staged a series of literary launches. Howard Junker, editor of *ZYZZYVA*, a San Francisco literary magazine, shares the enthusiasm: 'it's a beautiful place and we're excited about doing readings, a salon or lunches there'. Kenneth Howe, writer for the *Chronicle*, sums it up when he says that the Rex 'goes big on ambience'.

Anyone familiar with the other hotels owned by the Joie de Vivre group, such as the Phoenix (also a Hip Hotel), will recognize Chip Conley's distinctive and idiosyncratic approach to the hotel business. Joie de Vivre's founding proprietor has thrived with a small hotel development formula that is all about targeting a niche within a niche. The Rex is

for writers and the Phoenix is for rockers – or, perhaps rather more accurately, the Rex is for writers, bibliophiles and would-be writers, while the Phoenix is for people who are in, or would love to be in, the music industry. This projection of our wishes and desires is certainly not a new discovery in marketing. The fashion industry, for one, has been doing it for years. But Conley is among the first to apply the approach to the marketing of small hotels.

Yet anyone who instinctively cringes at the thought of a themed hotel should not be put off. This is theme, not theme park; Hotel Rex is most definitely not 'à la Disney'. Designers Ted Boerner and Candra Scott (who also created the interior of Portland's Governor Hotel) have resorted to nothing more tricky than old books, old paintings and big old club chairs to evoke an atmosphere unanimously (and surprisingly romantically) described in the American media as an authentic 'literary lair'.

address Hotel Rex, 562 Sutter Street, San Francisco, California 94102, USA
t +1 (415) 433 4434 **f** +1 (415) 433 3695 **e** rexres@jdvhospitality.com
room rates from US$195

lydmar hotel

There's something particularly appropriate about the fact that Per Lydmar, the founder of this hotel in Stockholm, is thinking about opening a place in Miami. The two cities have more in common than most people might possibly imagine. Weather is without question *not* one of them. But instead of temperature, the cities share a common temperament. Like Miami, Stockholm is a newly discovered metropolis. Where Miami has salsa, Stockholm has jazz. Where Miami people look good parading around Ocean Drive without much on, the hip young things on Sturegatan look equally good in their cold-weather utility chic.

Like Miami, Stockholm is built in and around the water, and although the Baltic may not be quite as inviting as the warm Atlantic, it does make this a beautiful city. One of the attractions of Stockholm is that it's a big city that gives the impression of being small. In atmosphere and lifestyle it resembles Amsterdam, despite having three times the population. It also doesn't hurt that Stockholm has resisted the attractions of the high-rise office block. The cityscape has thus remained on a scale more like that of Paris. Add to this the fact that Stockholm is nowhere near as prohibitively expensive as, say, London, and

it's understandable that it should have become an urban travel hotspot with foreigners and Swedes alike.

No hotel complements the new Stockholm better than Lydmar. It's not just a hotel with a popular bar and a couple of really good restaurants, it's a hangout − a place to drop in and listen to some live music, an ideal venue for a coffee on the way to work or a drink on the way home. Like the Bleibtreu in Berlin, the Costes in Paris or the Mercer in New York, you need never leave the premises to feel that you are truly in the heart of the city.

In design, the guest rooms are such that you may not want to leave your room, let alone the hotel. For pricing purposes, they have been simplified to a t-shirt formula of small, medium, large and extra large. But that's about all they have in common. Otherwise they are all different. That in itself is nothing particularly new, but what does distinguish the Lydmar interiors is that they have been executed not just with style, flair and a feel for the contemporary pulse, but also with a quite extraordinary respect for quality. From the joinery to the taps to the light switches, the tiling and the bedside lamps, everything is substantial and exceptionally well made.

223

Located in the centre of Stockholm, Lydmar is better known to locals as a bar and restaurant than as a hotel

Original, colourful, funky – apart from the latest TV and music systems, every room is different

Lydmar proves the maxim that hotels are the new nightclubs. It is a magnet for the chic youth of Stockholm

Unexpected details such as this rather baroque damask-silk patchwork quilt give the rooms individuality

The building was designed in the 1960s for the Stockholm Exhibition. Only part of it has been turned to a hotel

White floors, orange walls, contemporary ceramics – there was never any question of playing it safe

The atmosphere is laid back. Chefs take their breaks in a corner of the restaurant; no nasty staff cafeteria here

Because it was designed for offices, the building has lots of windows – a big plus during the dark Scandinavian winter

As at 'Spoon' in Paris, you select a main dish and then pick accompanying dishes according to your own taste

Contemporary simplicity combines with the odd splash of rich colour and sumptuous sheen and texture

The atmosphere in the restaurant and bar is more Barcelona than Scandinavia; the food is a mix of Asia and Italy

The general design theme of strong modernity continues in the immaculate bathrooms

No boring corridors for this hotel. One landing features a grand piano topped by a vase of pussy willow

Rooms are graded like t-shirts: small, medium, large, extra-large. This penthouse loft is extra-large

Dinner is accompanied by live jazz and soul, while the restaurant walls exhibit works of contemporary art

Many hotels claim that their rooms are all different, but at Lydmar this really is true; only the fine quality is standard

People drop in all day long for coffee, breakfast, lunch, a drink or just to listen to some jazz

Tiny touches of pink and blue add an unpredictable element to an all-white room that is perfect for a Swedish winter

The TVs are the latest flat-screened models, the telephones are the most sophisticated on the market, the furniture is all from leading Italian manufacturers. Nowhere is there evidence of skimping, and everywhere there is proof of an almost obsessive attention to detail.

Like the Pelican in Miami, Lydmar Hotel has no lobby. There's a corner of the restaurant where people check in, but calling it a lobby is a big stretch. At first this is a bit disconcerting, especially if you find yourself bumping into people enjoying an after-work drink as you drag your bags to what you think might be the reception. But once you are settled with a Tall Sea Breeze the vision of the next bewildered guests trying to make their way through is rather entertaining. Conversely, there are quite a few locals who mistakenly queue at reception to order their next drink.

What I like most of all about Lydmar is its ability to combine relaxed with refined. Though the hotel has the head lease on the building, many floors are shared with business and professional addresses. For some hotels it might be a problem that guest rooms are mixed with doctor's surgeries or that one floor has a resident orthodontist. At Lydmar this only seems to add to its street cred. The fact that an elderly lady dressed in a fur coat is late for an appointment with her psychiatrist and that not everyone is dressed in standard-issue black makes the place real and gives it charm.

To my mind the most graphic example of Lydmar's attitude is the elevator music. Nothing special to look at, the lift features a panel of buttons for choosing not what floor to go to but what to listen to on the way. Options include soul, acid jazz, R 'n' B, pop, classical and ambient. Suddenly you find yourself wishing your room was on a higher floor. Banishing the normal drone of elevator music is like cutting the last shackle of conformity. It's Lydmar's way of saying 'as far as we're concerned the rule is that there are no rules'. Even in Miami, the lifts haven't come this far.

address Lydmar Hotel, Sturegatan 10, S-114 36 Stockholm, Sweden
t +46 (8) 5661 1300 **f** +46 (8) 5661 1301 **e** info@lydmar.se
room rates from SEK 1225

establishment

Sydney is a tough city to do business in. Who wants to work when the harbour and beaches are only minutes away? Yet there are plenty for whom surf, sand and sailing are not on the agenda. Sydney after all is a city of five million people and the commercial heart of Australia.

If you must work, then you also must stay at Establishment. For despite being in the heart of the business district, just behind the Stock Exchange, Establishment is anything but. This is without doubt the most fun and the most decadent place to stay in Sydney. Why? Because it has turned the 'hotel with trendy bar' concept on its head. Establishment is not a hip hotel with a hot bar; it's a hot bar, a trend-setting club, the city's best sushi bar and one of its most talked-about restaurants – all of which happen to have a nice little hotel attached.

Not that the hotel part of Establishment was – or feels like – an afterthought. The loft-like guest rooms are sumptuously spacious, with open-plan bathrooms. And they're equipped like lofts, with Bang & Olufsen stereos, internet television, state-of-the-art Vola bathroom fittings, and acres of built-in storage. There are two decorative options: a light version that's all silvery and dove-grey – the interior equivalent of a Prada summer suit –

and more urban rooms with rugged dark wooden floors and exposed beams – more the after-hours Dolce & Gabbana version.

Tempting as these spacious settings are for room service and a movie … don't. You'd be missing out on the giant adult funfair that is Establishment. The front bar – the best in town – is so hot that it has to employ bouncers to keep people out. This despite the fact that it's the longest bar in the whole of Australia. As a hotel guest you have no such problem – you have your own entrance. Then there's the Est restaurant on the first floor, currently *the* chic place to eat. And the handy in-house hedonism doesn't end there. The entire top floor of this substantial Victorian building has been converted to a private Moroccan-themed bar, complete with one of the best sushi restaurants in town. And to top it off, for those really determined not to go back to their rooms, there's the chic sixties-style Tank nightclub in the three-level basement, which is – yes, you guessed it – currently the hottest ticket in town.

None of this, of course, came about by accident. Opened in 2000, Establishment was the creation of Sydney's most experienced and consistently successful style dynasty.

Merivale and Mr John, trademarks of founders John and Merivale Hemmes, were synonymous with *au courant* in seventies Australia – the Biba of the Antipodes. At a time when, to Brits at least, Australia was still the land of Barry Humphries, John and Merivale Hemmes were dressing the more adventurous residents – and rock stars – in outfits that could compete with David Bowie's Aladdin Zane. They were first with snakeskin platform shoes and super-flared trousers – and that was just for men. But unlike Biba, they did not fall into terminal decline when times and fashions changed. Instead, John and Merivale simply shifted to hospitality.

First they converted a Sydney boutique to a tearoom, and then in time added a lunchtime restaurant. Gradually the family expanded into more restaurants and bars, and eventually a hotel. But none of this happened overnight. In fact the years between the opening of the first lunchroom and the launch of Establishment spanned the entire childhood of their son and daughter. By the turn of the twenty-first century, the next generation of Hemmeses were ready to take the reins. It was Justin Hemmes who convinced the family to take on the task of restoring the old city landmark of George Patterson House. The building, distinguished by a pressed-tin ceiling and elaborate cast-iron columns, was at one time the headquarters of Australia's foremost advertising agency. By the time it was purchased by the Hemmes clan, it had been ravaged by fire and half was missing. To their credit they decided to leave it that way – at least in part – simply covering over the burned-out bit with a modern glass roof to form the Garden Bar and leaving it at that. The stamp of several generations of style is everywhere evident. In the Moroccan-inspired Hemmesphere private bar, for instance, the mood is one of relaxed ethno-chic. Culturally speaking, the turnaround is extraordinary. If you had said to an Aussi thirty years ago that a front bar in Sydney would have more women than men on a Friday night, the bloke would have declared you Aladdin Zane.

---

address Establishment, 5 Bridge Lane, Sydney 2000, NSW, Australia

t +61 (2) 9240 3000 **f** +61 (2) 9240 3001 **e** info@establishmenthotel.com

room rates from A$290

park hyatt

Tokyo has an edge – even the most seasoned, globetrotting journo would agree that this is one of the most exotic locations on the planet.

It's not exotic in a 'tigers in the jungle, naked sirens under the waterfalls' kind of way, but rather in the sense that everything is different – *so* different. Compared to the Big Apple's neatly numbered grid of skyscrapers, or LA's clearly defined collection of freeways, Tokyo is chaos. Even the higgledy-piggledy arrangement of London's streets is positively rational compared to Tokyo's grimy maze of lanes and alleyways. Tokyo taxi drivers are reluctant to venture out of their specific zones and frequently get hopelessly lost. If you lose the card that has the name and address of your hotel printed in Japanese, you are in trouble.

Most mystifying of all is the fact that the city did not have to be this way. There was not a lot of it left after World War II and it could have modelled itself on any metropolis, real or ideal. Instead, it grew organically into a larger, denser version of its former feudal self. The longer you stay in Tokyo the stranger it all gets. The differences are embedded in the very detail of everyday life: books and magazines are read from back to front; everyone (especially grown-ups) is obsessed with comic

books; officials or quasi-officials (including taxi drivers) all wear white cotton gloves; and everything, even a solitary grapefruit, is wrapped as if it were a wedding present. Then there's the vast human tide of commuters. The metro at rush hour couldn't function without its professional pushers, whose job is – quite literally – to push as many people on to a train as possible before the doors close.

To Western eyes, Tokyo remains far more enigmatic than most global capitals. Apart from the nocturnal neon spectacle and gaudy pachinko pin-ball parlours, few visitors have a clear vision of what to expect. Preconceptions run from romanticized Blade Runner scenarios to a more sinister Yakuza version populated by Samurai bikers in black leather.

Truth be known, architecturally speaking, Tokyo is quite a disappointment; a grim, grey maze of pock-marked concrete with just the odd design showpiece thrown in. It certainly doesn't give off much futuristic gleam. There's a 'let it crumble' attitude – perhaps because whatever they build, an earthquake is sure to come along every six decades or so to knock it all down. But there is an upside to the 'quake town' mentality – lack of permanence means developers are willing to be more adventurous.

This accounts for a lot, including the fact that the Tokyo Park Hyatt is by far the most avant-garde hotel in the international Hyatt chain. Like its host city, it has an edge. The hotel occupies the top fourteen floors of veteran Japanese architect Kenzo Tange's Shinjuku Park Tower – starting on floor thirty-nine. Putting a hotel fifty storeys up in one of the world's most earthquake-prone cities is a gutsy move. The reward for refusing to be intimated by Mother Nature is the amazing view. From the double-height windows of the fifty-first floor New York Grill you can see Mount Fuji in the far distance and, by night, Tokyo neon glamour at its most spectacular.

The hotel, situated beneath the summit of three interlocking towers, is a distillation of all that makes Tokyo different and exciting. The tell-tale attention to detail is evident in the laundry that is returned wrapped in fine handmade paper, or the immaculate delicacies delivered by kimono-clad staff on handmade plates and bowls. Tokyo's preoccupation with food reflects in the wide choice on offer: the New York Grill serves state-of-the-art crossover East-West fusion cuisine; then there is Girandole, serving Continental fare in a double-height space decorated with a gigantic collage of photographs of café life in Europe; and finally Kozue, the in-house Japanese restaurant in a timber-panelled double-height modernist space.

Tokyo's reputation as a shopper's paradise is upheld by the range of stores immediately downstairs, including that beacon of hip contemporary luxury, the Conran Shop. The top-floor health club is a sensation, complete with a swimming pool set underneath the intersecting planes of the roof. A 14,000-volume library offers an almost Zen-like retreat. Guestrooms are spacious and elegantly minimal, with Japanese rice paper lamps and select works by master ceramists. It's not surprising that *Wallpaper* recently elected the hotel rooms in this Shinjuku landmark as the best on the planet.

---

address Park Hyatt, 3-7-1-2 Nishi-Shinjuku, Shinjuku-ku, Tokyo 163-1055, Japan

t +81 (3) 5322 1234 **f** +81 (3) 5322 1288

room rates from 49,000 Yen

das triest

In a city heavy with history, Das Triest is a light interlude. City of dancing horses, cosy cafés, *Sacher Torte* and Mozart, Vienna is steeped in history like few others. And unlike their Italian neighbours, the Austrians do not have the temperament to toss aside the baggage of history with a nonchalant shrug. In true eastern European fashion, heritage is taken as a weighty, serious affair. As former seat of the Hapsburg dynasty, this city, on the border of eastern and western Europe, has played a significant role in just about every event that has shaped the modern world. From its defeat of the all-conquering Ottoman Turks – knocking on the city's gates in the sixteenth and seventeenth centuries – to its pivotal role in the eruption of World War I, Vienna has seen and done it all. And it shows. There's scarcely a corner, square, park or avenue that is not adorned with a commemorative statue, bust, fountain or sculpture.

That's what makes this hotel such a welcome addition to Vienna. Das Triest is light and easy going – quite a contrast in a city where traditional Tyrolean costume (the kind worn by the entire von Trapp family in *The Sound of Music*) is still displayed in the window of every other 'fashion' shop. Das Triest is

a chance to throw that burdensome mantle of history onto a designer chair in the corner.

This hotel is an indirect result of the fall of the Iron Curtain. A decade ago, Vienna was suddenly no longer positioned on the outer fringe of a handful of repressed and politically estranged nations. Instead, it was the first and most conveniently located western city for its recently liberated eastern neighbours. With the collapse of Communism, Vienna emerged as a newly fashioned 'Hapsburg hub', springboard to the rapidly emerging markets of Hungary, Slovakia, Poland and the Czech Republic. It was in this dynamic climate that Dr Alexander Maculan identified a major gap in the Viennese market: the need for a hotel catering to a taste for civilized chic. If Vienna was going to make a serious bid to establish itself as the creative centre of eastern Europe, then it must attract art directors, ad agencies, photographers, stylists and so on – and if so, then it better have somewhere for them to stay.

The partners at first struggled to pinpoint the right approach for the hotel's interior: the proposals were all either too stark or too fussy. Until, that is, they were having dinner one night in Quaglino's in London. There they were inspired by Terence Conran's massive space.

The fireplace in the salon of Das Triest
is particularly inviting during
the cold Viennese winter

Overlooking the courtyard, the hotel
restaurant serves a modern version
of traditional Austrian dishes

The bar, a popular after-work meeting
place, has the leather-upholstered
intimacy of a private railway carriage

White bedlinen and cherry wood
furniture define the warm but
unmistakably modern rooms

The concierge desk in the black and
white entrance – a classic example
of Terence Conran's design

A beautifully sculptural staircase
leads from the lobby to each
of the hotel's seven floors

They immediately decided to invite Conran to Vienna to do the same with their property. He gave them just the look they wanted – modern but not hard. With warm cherry wood and furniture upholstered in bright shades of blue, red, yellow and green, he created a sense of comfort that offsets the acres of white walls.

Not that Das Triest has turned its back on history. Built in the mid-seventeenth century just outside the city gates, it was a hostelry during Austria's imperial reign, accommodating the footmen and horses of the royal mail coach en route to Austria's only seaport, Trieste (hence the hotel's name). The salon retains the original vaulted ceilings of the royal stables. Divided into separate areas by gilded folding screens, the various vaulted conversation spaces of the lobby offer intimacy and privacy. And the restaurant, a long rectangular space with a view of the courtyard garden, has done with the food what the building has done with the architecture, serving a lighter, less self-conscious version of Viennese tradition.

The tribute to Vienna's glorious history continues with the black-and-white prints throughout the hotel by Viennese photographer Christine de Grancy. Her photos capture the city's spectacular array of busts and statues from a roof-top perspective: an appropriate introduction to Vienna's architectural triumphs. And given its location, Das Triest is a great place from which to take in the real thing. The view from the top-floor terrace offers a panorama of the city's monuments, most spectacularly the brightly coloured mosaic roof of St Stephen's, the Gothic cathedral.

When you weary of the spectacle of Vienna's treasures, there is always the spectacle of the scene in the hotel. At night Das Triest really comes alive. Here one can see the truth of Ian Schrager's claim that hotels are the new nightclubs. All of Vienna seems to hang out here, spilling out from the bar into the lobby and restaurant in a ritual that comes close to a nightly full-blown party. As a guest you never need be on the outside looking in.

---

address Das Triest, Wiedner Hauptstrasse 12, 1040 Vienna, Austria

t +43 (1) 589 18 0   **f** +43 (1) 589 18 18   **e** back@dastriest.at

room rates from EUR 175

widder hotel

Just off the famous Bahnhofstrasse in the very heart of old Zurich there is a picturesque little side street called the Rennweg. It is packed with boutiques and restaurants and delicious little pastry and chocolate shops, just like Swiss streets are supposed to be. It is only after walking straight past yet another seventeenth-century picture-postcard shop front that you realize you've just missed the entrance to Zurich's most celebrated new hotel, the Widder.

This is definitely *not* what you would expect from a five-star hotel located in the centre of a major city, especially a Swiss city. But then the Widder is unlike any other hotel. It's not just the entrance that is disguised on this charming shopping street: the entire hotel is completely hidden within a complex of houses dating back as far as the eleventh and twelfth centuries. From the street it is difficult to discern the presence of any hotel at all.

In all, Widder Hotel comprises ten different historic houses, beginning on the Rennweg and bending around the corner into the Augustinerstrasse. Originally owned separately by feudal guilds, the properties were purchased collectively by the Union Bank of Switzerland in 1970 as an investment. Faced with a property of paramount historical sensitivity,

a special preservation committee was established which eventually selected Tilla Theuss as the architect who would convert the properties collectively into a modern hotel. And what a task! A bigger bureaucratic hurdle is hard to imagine. Not every member of the city council thought this project was such a great idea (no surprise) and the job got even harder when initial work uncovered priceless sixteenth-century frescoes, rare river-stone floors, precious painted ceilings and an original city wall dating from the twelfth century. Not only did each new archaeological discovery have to be incorporated into the overall scheme, but work slowed to a crawl in fear of damaging some other as-yet-undiscovered remnant. Add to this the fact that the ten houses had somehow to be united as a single unit without altering the individual structure of each and it's hardly surprising that this ambitious project ended up taking more than ten years in planning and construction.

In the end, Theuss allowed the history and experience of each individual house to determine the design. The Augustiner House, for example, is decorated in Biedermeier fashion, while the interior of the Pferch House is seventeenth-century Baroque, and so on.

A room in the Biedermeier style in the Augustiner House, one of ten individual houses comprising Widder Hotel

Rustic hand-painted local antiques are combined with modern classics throughout the hotel

The mezzanine of this seemingly modern, loft-like space is an unexpected find in a seventeenth-century building

Ornate painted murals were uncovered by accident during the early stages of the construction work

Eames chairs, a modern fireplace, a mosaic terrazzo floor and original river-stone walls define the lobby bar

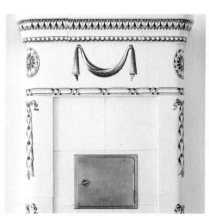

The Biedermeier ceramic stove was one of many historic treasures saved during the renovation of these old city houses

In summer, the outdoor terrace adjoining the lobby is a pleasant surprise in the heart of old Zurich

An original sixteenth-century mural contrasts with the modern furniture of the Augustiner House

Situated on a quaint shopping street in the historic city centre, it's impossible to tell from the outside that this is a hotel

The painted beams of the Widder's private dining room are sixteenth-century originals

Breakfast is served in the high-tech atrium, whose cantilevered glass roof opens in the summer

Some of the fragments of wall murals date back as far as the thirteenth century

The duplex rooms of the Pfeife House are uncompromising in their modernity

Even the Widder's meeting rooms feature the results of the hotel's ten-year renovation

The dark panelling and sombre tones of the furniture are in keeping with the style of the Pferch House

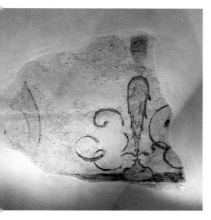

Renovation work progressed slowly because of the chance of uncovering fragments of historic frescoes

Tucked into the basement is the Widder Bar, one of Zurich's hottest jazz clubs

The view from the terrace of the Widderzunft House, with Lake Zurich in the background

The result is a bewildering variety of architectural and decorative styles which, coupled with the complexity of links joining the ten different houses, has created a veritable design labyrinth. Every corridor and staircase leads to yet another unexpected room or space, in yet another architectural style and mood. And there are corridors and staircases everywhere. The intricacy of the overall structure makes it easy to lose your way. Even after studying the plan closely, I couldn't work it out. But I like it that way. The whole notion of hidden places and spaces evokes childhood memories of playing in the attic – the fun is in *not* knowing what you'll find. Anyone who relishes the unexpected and abhors predictability will definitely love it here.

So too will the design aficionado. This hotel is a furniture lover's paradise. Every famous piece of modern furniture by the biggest names in design and architecture is here – somewhere. Le Corbusier, Mies van der Rohe, Adolf Loos, Charles and Ray Eames, Eileen Gray, Josef Hoffmann, Frank Lloyd Wright, Mario Bellini, Harry Bertoia … the list goes on. This feast of modern classics is distributed throughout the hotel, helping to bridge the hundreds of years of different history and heritage it encompasses.

Needless to say, each and every one of Widder Hotel's forty-two rooms and seven suites is completely different. In an ideal world, as a guest, you would select the fantasy and style that appeals most. In reality, Widder Hotel is far too popular for you to be able to do this, so the policy is good old-fashioned pot luck. But this works surprisingly well, challenging guests to experience environments that often challenge and change their preconceived opinions.

For the reader concerned at what may sound like very 'un-Swiss' randomness, complexity and unpredictability … do not fret! Widder Hotel has earned its five stars the hard way, by providing standards of service that are typically Swiss – i.e. immaculate.

address Widder Hotel, Rennweg 7, CH–8001 Zurich, Switzerland
t +41 (1) 224 25 26   **f** +41 (1) 224 24 24   **e** home@widderhotel.ch
room rates from 395 SFr

Photography by Herbert Ypma, with the exception
of the Sukhothai, the Hempel and Widder Hotel, all
generously supplied by the hotels.

First published in the United States of America in
1999 by Thames & Hudson Inc., 500 Fifth Avenue,
New York, New York 10110

New edition 2001

Library of Congress Catalog Card Number
2001086852
ISBN 0-500-28301-X

Designed by Maggi Smith

Printed and bound in Singapore by CS Graphics